The SENCO Handbook
Working within a whole-school approach

Personal Copy

ELIZABETH A. COWNE

David Fulton Publishers
London

David Fulton Publishers Ltd
2 Barbon Close, London WC1N 3JX

First published in Great Britain by
David Fulton Publishers 1996

Note: The right of Elizabeth Cowne to be identified as the author of this work has been asserted by her in accordance with the Copyright, Designs and Patents Act 1988.

Copyright © Elizabeth A. Cowne

British Library Cataloguing in Publication Data

A catalogue record for this book is available from the British Library

ISBN 1-85346-413-9

All rights reserved. No part of this publication may be reproduced, stored in a retrieval system or transmitted in any form, or by any means, electronic, mechanical, photocopying, recording or otherwise, without the prior permission of the publishers.

Typeset by The Harrington Consultancy
Printed in Great Britain by Bell & Bain Ltd

Contents

Acknowledgements		4
Foreword		5
How to use this book		6
1.	Decisions and Dilemmas in SEN: Legislative and Historical Legacies	8
2.	Roles and Responsibilities for SEN within a Whole-school Policy	15
3.	Identification and Intervention: the Individual Education Plan	23
4.	The Curriculum: Whatever Happened to Differentiation?	35
5.	The Curriculum: Key Issues for Key Stages	47
6.	Managing Effective Support	55
7.	Multi-professional Networks	64
8.	Paperwork and Procedures: the Co-ordinating Role	78
9.	Supporting Others: the Consultancy Role	88
10.	The Role of the SENCO: Working within a Whole-school Approach	99

Activity Pack	1. Roles and Responsibilities: exercise	104
	2. Audit of Whole-school Policy	106
	3. Lesson Planning for Differentiation	109
	4. Room Management: exercise	112
	5. Information Flow for IEPs: exercise	116
	6. Reviewing Parental Policy	118
Source Lists	1. Assessment: tools and resources for teaching	120
	2. Further reading: disabilities, difficulties, policy, training	121
	3. Addresses of Voluntary Organisations	123
Appendices	**Note:** The appendices are numbered as they relate to the numbered chapters.	
	1. Categories of disabilities used by LEAs from 1959	126
	2a. Governors' Responsibilities (from the Code of Practice)	126
	2b. Schedule 1: Reg 2 (1) Whole-school Policy Information	127
	3a. Guidance notes on Code of Practice forms	128
	3b. Bilingual Learners (notes)	131
	4a. Instrumental Enrichment (notes)	132
	4b. Bloom's Taxonomy (notes)	133
	8a. Appendices to Statements	134
	8b. The SEN Management Form	134
	9a. Observation (notes)	136
	9b. Questionnaire form	138
	9c. Parental responsibilities (from Children Act)	138
Bibliography		139
Index		143

Acknowledgements

The author would like to thank the very many colleagues who have contributed inspiration to, or direct advice on, the writing of this book. I owe the original idea for the book to Judith Jones, who edited, and all those colleagues in the Learning Support Group and Merton schools who contributed to, the Merton version of a SENCO Handbook, produced for our schools last year. I also acknowledge as one source of ideas, the Merton Guidelines (1991) on whole-school policy developed by Harriet Strickland, Paul Greenhalgh and our working party of teachers from Merton schools.

I also owe a debt to the hundreds of course members from all phases of education, and from most LEAs in the Greater London area, with whom I have worked since 1983. Their projects, on curriculum differentiation and other aspects of whole-school policy development, carried out as part of SENIOS or OU coursework, have given me in-depth knowledge of how SENCOs manage change. From small beginnings and working within many constraints, these teachers and thousands like them made it possible to have a Code built upon their good practice which benefits children with special educational needs in mainstream schools.

I would also like to thank the following individuals for their constructive criticism and advice about the chapters they read in draft: Hilary Lucas (Harrow), Linda Coventon (Lewisham SENCO), Janet Warner (Croydon SENCO), Linda Roberts, Christine Duckworth (members of the Merton LSS), Bernie Marcou (Merton SENCO), Sabina Melidi, John Brown (Head: Bromley). Also Trevor Cook, Paul Greenhalgh, Christine Clatworthy, Mary Hrekow, Susan Murray and Nick Peacey who helped with additional information and advice.

Crown copyright is reproduced with the permission of the Controller of HMSO.

My thanks go most to my daughter, Alison, for her hard work, patience and skill in producing the typed script and for making the production of the book possible. Thanks also to John, my partner, for his patient support and help.

Elizabeth Cowne
March 1996

Foreword

School SEN Co-ordinators (SENCOs) were once optional extras. Then the 1993 Education Act came along. Now virtually every school has a SEN Co-ordinator.

The legal and regulatory spotlight on the SENCO's role has shown that the women and men (far more women) holding these important posts are often working alone, or nearly alone. They need training, support and time to do the job.

The author of a book supporting the SENCO's work must be someone with great practical expertise and understanding of schools, a commitment to achieving the best for all pupils and the ability to take a broad view, both in relation to historical developments and national, local and individual school systems.

Liz Cowne meets all the criteria. She has a long background in mainstream school work with SEN, has been involved since 1983 in innovative teacher training for SENCOs at the Institute of Education, London University, and in Merton LEA, and still gives up her evenings for her voluntary work as the Chair of the Greater London branch of the National Association for Special Educational Needs.

The Education Act is now three years old. Liz Cowne has been able to review practice since 1993 nationally and across the many schools she knows well. She has drawn out the key issues and difficulties. She can offer full discussion of the issues and provide solutions that she has seen working in schools.

I particularly welcome the attention Liz Cowne gives to curriculum, both in its broadest sense and in the narrower definition delineated by the National Curriculum. If pupils with special educational needs are to achieve their entitlement from both the 1988 and 1993 Education Acts, a proper understanding of the place of every teacher and classroom in the task is essential.

Liz Cowne's ability to provide a theoretical context to practical ideas is shown at its best in her discussion of the role of the individual education plan in relation to whole curriculum design. She suggests that we need to be careful that a device for action on priorities for individuals does not draw us to a narrow viewpoint.

The SENCO, of course, is not just a hands-on operator. Through her skill in professional development and support other teachers grow and develop their practice in relation to special educational needs. Liz Cowne explores all this and, to offer support to supporters, presents some well tested staff models for readers to try.

I am delighted to introduce this book and its author to the reader. It will take her a few pages to show you what a good friend she is to those who take on the challenging task of SENCO – and to all those children and young people whose learning SENCOs seek to enhance.

Nick Peacey, SENJIT.
Institute of Education: London
January 1996

How to use this book

This book is intended to help SENCOs, heads and others to implement an effective policy for special educational needs in every school. Such people are busy, so may not read the book straight through. These guidance notes are to tell you how to find what you need and to link the themes which run through the chapters. The book begins with a debate on issues about SEN and their historic and legislative origins. This could be useful if you wish to get your staff to look at their concepts of special needs and the value systems of the school. The activities are all to be found in the Activity Pack (pp.104-19).

Chapter 1: Decisions and Dilemmas: Legislative and Historical Legacies

The purpose of this chapter is to outline the history of special needs legislation and practice, in order to examine changing perspectives and attitudes left as a legacy from the past. Disability issues run through this history, as does the changing role of schools, governors, parents and LEAs in relationship to children with special educational needs.

Chapter 2: Roles and Responsibilities for SEN within a Whole-school Policy

This chapter begins by outlining the roles of governors, head, SENCO and class teachers as described in the Code of Practice and in Circular 6/94. Next, the development of the SENCO role from 1983 to date is described. In particular the focus is on how SENCOs have been trained, using earmarked funds for Special Educational Needs in Ordinary Schools (SENIOS) courses. The content of this book has its origin in these courses, run by the author, based either at the Institute of Education, London or in LEA professional development centres. The chapter should be used in conjunction with **Activities 1 & 2**. **Source List 2** contains further reading.

Chapter 3: Identification and Intervention: The Individual Education Plan

This chapter looks at the role of SENCOs in relation to the maintenance of the SEN register, the identification of pupils at Stage 1 to 3 of the Code of Practice and the subsequent assessment and intervention programmes for all those on the register, including the writing of Individual Education Plans (IEPs). **IEP forms and guidance notes are included in Appendix 3. Source Lists 1 & 2** give further information about assessment and further reading. Descriptions of the work at Stages 4 and 5 and the overall management of files and reviews is continued in Chapter 8.

Chapter 4: The Curriculum: Whatever Happened to Differentiation?

This chapter introduces the theme of differentiation in conjunction with that of entitlement to the National Curriculum for all pupils. Three perspectives on differentiation are then considered: behavioural, cognitive and affective interventions.

Chapter 5: The Curriculum: Key Issues for Key Stages

This second chapter on the curriculum gives practical ideas for SENCOs to work with colleagues on differentiation in each of the National Curriculum Key Stages. **Activity 3** is a staff development exercise on lesson planning in any of Key Stages 1–3.

Chapter 6: Managing Effective Support

The theme of roles and responsibilities continues by considering in detail the responsibilities of managing support staff. This is frequently a role given to SENCOs. Different models of support are described; support for the child, the teacher, the curriculum and the family, to which is added support for the SENCO! **Activity 4** can be used to analyse effective classroom team-work. **Source List 2** gives information about training for Special Support Assistants.

Chapter 7: Multi-professional Networks

This chapter looks at one of the key roles of SENCOs: to build relationships with outside services and agencies, other schools and the networks of voluntary organisations. Partnership with other professionals at critical transition points in the pupils' careers is also described: e.g., entry to school, phase transfer, the transition plan at 14+. **Source List 3** contains useful addresses of voluntary organisations.

Chapter 8: Paperwork and Procedures: the Co-ordinating Role

The bureaucratic role of the SENCO is discussed; including such essential duties as maintaining the SEN register, running IEP reviews and annual reviews for those with statements. This chapter is concerned mainly with the SENCO's role between Stage 3 and Stages 4 and 5 and with other quasi-legal aspects: e.g., tribunals and inspections. It should be read in conjunction with Chapter 3. **Activity 5** is designed to help larger schools look at information flow in and out of the Learning Support Department.

Chapter 9: Supporting Others: the Consultancy Role

This chapter considers three aspects of the SENCO's role, working with children, parents and teachers and links this to the roles discussed in other chapters. **Activity 6** (using the same structure as Activity 2) reviews the school's policy for working with parents. **Appendix 9** contains notes on observation methods and other ideas for understanding the pupil's perspective.

Chapter 10: The Role of the SENCO: Working within a Whole-school Approach

The totality of the role of the SENCO is explored and models for rethinking this role are suggested. Special educational needs as a construct within whole-school effectiveness is discussed. Ways of evaluating policies are suggested which aim at effective inclusive education for all.

CHAPTER 1

Decisions and Dilemmas in Special Educational Needs: Legislative and Historical Legacies

The 1944 Act stated that LEAs should 'secure that provision is made for pupils who suffer from any disability of mind or body, by providing either in special schools or otherwise, special educational treatment, that is to say education by special methods for persons suffering from that disability.'

The 1981 Act redefined the population of pupils with disabilities as those with 'special educational needs.' This Act gave clear guidelines about assessment procedures and the issuing of a statement of special educational needs. Building on the recommendations of the Warnock report, much was said about involving parents in the decision-making processes at all stages. Head teachers and governors had clear duties to identify and meet the needs of pupils with special educational needs.

The term 'special educational needs' depends not only on a concept of discontinuity of provision, but also on the concept of relativity of need. This is the most fundamental dilemma of special educational needs, because although the term includes children with disabilities, it also includes those whose educational progress in learning is significantly slower than that of their peer group, for whatever cause. To identify which individuals have such needs and so require something extra or something different from what is normally provided, requires a decision-making process.

Resource levels

Extra resourcing for special educational needs makes assumptions about what constitutes normal provision across schools or local authorities. Schools, particularly since the Education Reform Act and local management of schools (LMS), have different levels of resourcing. Schools differ in the amounts allocated to their special educational needs budget. How can funds be shared within and between schools and across Local Education Authorities (LEAs) in a way which will help even out what is provided 'normally'? How can schools allocate funds between and amongst their pupils with special educational needs in an equitable manner?

As well as a discontinuity principle in special educational needs, there is also a continuity of need between what is perceived as special or normal. The graduation is such that the cut-off point can be arbitrary, or appear so. The decision as to where to make this cut-off of definitions of need, is made by a range of individuals and organisations. All of these have differing perspectives about their priorities, which depend on their knowledge and their value systems. This presents the second dilemma of special educational needs. Everyone has a different construct of the term 'special educational needs,' which then relates to different priorities about how to use available resources to meet these needs. As Tomlinson (1982) remarks:

> The history of special education must be viewed in terms of the benefits it brought for a developing industrial society, the benefits for the normal mass education system of a special sub-system of education, and the benefits that medical, psychological and educational personnel derive from encouraging new areas of professional expertise.

(p.29)

Who will benefit from present day decisions about policies and resources for special educational needs?

Multi-professional decision making

The more complex a child's need the more people will be involved in the decision-making process, within and across organisations and professions. Communication between these individuals and organisations is important, if coherent and consistent decisions are to be made.

The power base of those who make such decisions has changed across the century. In the earliest decades, the medical profession, often alone, chose which child went to a special school or indeed had any schooling at all. The LEA was intended to ascertain which children needed special treatment and decide on placement according to category. The advice used to make this decision came largely from medical officers (see Appendix 1). Sutton (1982) states that

> For years, it remained unclear who were the gate keepers to special education and despite the law's clear statement that the final decision lay with the LEA, in practice the actual decision very often lay with a medical officer following prescribed procedures. (p.11)

In the middle decades, decisions began to be shared, psychologists began to be employed to test the group of children seen as backward and to assist the medical officers in their decision making. An IQ test was the most frequently used measure to ascertain which children were 'educationally sub-normal.' However, it was also recognised that a variety of causes could contribute to backwardness.

Towards the end of the period 1944–1978, much had changed. A complex special education system of schools, classes and services had been built up. Teacher training and specialisms had also developed. Children with severe learning difficulties were at last given the right to education through the Handicapped Children Act (1970). Parents had begun, through voluntary groups, to exert pressure for change. Influences from abroad (the USA in particular) were affecting the thinking of such parent groups.

The 1981 Act

The 1981 Act gave great value to multi-disciplinary assessment. The power of the medical profession and its model, which had affected special education for so long, was reduced. The focus was on educational needs and these were to be described in educational terms and met by educational provision. Treatment was not a word used in describing this provision. Guidance on assessment and statements was given through Circular 1/83.

The 1981 Act required joint decision-making between health, education and social services. Goucher *et al* (1988) found that the frames of references of those who identified and described SEN problems came largely from the medical, educational and social work professionals. The researchers felt that professionals influenced the shaping of the policy in practice, but that parents had a role to challenge these influences. Parents began to have more say in their child's assessment and voluntary organisations began to lobby on behalf of different groups of children.

Cross-professional priorities

Provision is made across what Fish (1989) called dimensions of need, all of which lie on a continuum. Decision-making becomes complex when the providers of different resources have different priorities. Education, for example, may specify that health authorities should provide therapies for children with SEN, but health may not see this as a priority area for their resources. This is a further dilemma which arises between cross-professional provision: one which must be resolved on a regional or national level.

The 1981 Act embodied much of what had been developing over time and could be perceived as a summary of 'best practice.' The 1981 Act influenced attitudes of teachers in mainstream schools. They began to recognise that pupils with SEN were their responsibility. Integration policies were adopted by many school and LEAs. Training for special needs in mainstream schools was funded through training grants from 1983 onwards. (DES Circulars 3/83-86)

The Education Reform Act

The Education Reform Act (1988) also contributed to the thinking about pupils with learning difficulties. This Act states that all children have a right to a 'broad, balanced, relevant and differentiated curriculum.' On the positive side this meant all pupils now had an 'entitlement curriculum.' On the negative side teachers were overloaded by the requirement to teach the number of subjects specified and to test and assess pupils' progress in all of these subjects. Schools began to be more aware of their overall performance as judged by these tests. Pupils with special educational needs were not always seen as an asset when comparative tables of results were produced. LMS meant that money followed pupils and the school roll defined the overall resources available. Special needs pupils might use more of these resources than the school wished.

The Children Act (1989)

This Act, though not focused on education, was influential in changing viewpoints about children's rights and parental responsibilities. The Act also influenced thinking about these rights within the 1993 Education Act and the Code of Practice.

Audit Commission Reports

In 1992, HMI and the Audit Commission published two papers related to special educational needs. The first of these; *Getting in on the Act*, reviewed the working of the 1981 Act and the way LEAs had met its objectives. It was mainly about issuing statements and the provision for pupils with SEN. It found that there was a lack of clarity and consistency over the thresholds which warranted the issuing of a statement for SEN. This was accompanied by *Getting the Act Together, A Management Handbook for Schools and LEAs*. This gave information about what was considered as good practice or suggested issues for consideration. These reports provided clarification about the respective roles of schools and LEAs and the need for more accountability for the provision given through a statement. These two papers influenced the subsequent framing of the 1993 Act and in particular the Code of Practice.

The 1993 Act and Code of Practice

The 1993 Education Act, Part 3, replaced much of the 1981 legislation without significant changes. The new elements were the setting up of the SEN Tribunal and the publishing of the Code of Practice on Identification and Assessment of Special Educational Needs. This document has a status between a regulation, which is mandatory, and a circular which is advisory. Schools and LEAs are required to use their best endeavours to meet with the requirements of the Code of Practice to make provision for pupils with SEN. However, certain parts are mandatory regulations.

The 1993 Act and Code of Practice have pushed the decision-making further towards schools and parents, but final decisions are still made by the LEAs, who take advice from other professionals through the multi-disciplinary assessment. Parents can and do initiate requests for assessment and have an increasing amount of power when exercised through the SEN tribunal and litigation, although only a few use this route.

Triggers for assessment

To help schools reach a consistent decision as to who has special needs, many LEAs have begun to devise sets of descriptions of various levels of need along the continuum. Points along this continuum have descriptors which guide decisions about the different stages of assessment and provision. These attempts to show both continuity and discontinuity across the dimensions of need are still developmental. They depend on the evidence-base about the pupil's needs or lack of progress and action taken. Some LEAs conduct an audit or moderation of the staged procedure to assist this process or help refine resourcing levels.

Although the Code of Practice uses the general term 'special educational needs', in Section 3 Par 3.55 – 3.94 there are descriptions of the eight common categories of need. It seems that ways of talking about different kinds of needs are necessary. There is a fear of labelling pupils, but the use of SEN as an adjective is itself a label and not always a positive one.

The original idea of the 1981 Act was not to increase the number of pupils with statements by including those with needs who were already in mainstream schools. In the past these pupils were often referred to a 'remedial department' in the school or given help by 'remedial teachers', usually help with reading and writing. Pressure from schools managing their budgets under constraints, along with the more competitive ethos of education, has put pressure on LEAs to give statements to a larger percentage of the population than had originally been intended. *The Act Moves on* (HMI, Audit Commission 1994) strongly advises LEAs to establish such triggers to help clarify decision-making about which pupils may require a statement of SEN.

Evidence of need

The concept of evidence through examples of pupil's work and successes, required by both the National Curriculum and Records of Achievement, is one of which schools are becoming more aware. However, evidence for special educational needs has a different quality from what is expected for these other purposes. It must include records of what is being done in the present situation to assist a pupil to meet the demands of the curriculum. Implicit in this evidence-gathering is the notion of review and monitoring over time, to see how the pupil responds to interventions and support. Decision-making about an individual's special educational needs is beginning to be related to the process of assessment and intervention *over time*, instead of a single assessment made by one or more professionals.

More than one professional group may take part in the process, including the parents and the pupil. Thus, not only has the power base of the decision-making process for SEN changed, but the evidence-base is changing in quite a radical manner. The dilemma now is about how much to concentrate on 'within child' factors, or how much to take account of the curriculum and the whole context in which the child is found.

Flexible resource management

Within the organisation of a school or LEA there must be decision-making processes for identifying and assessing needs. This requires policies on how such needs are to be met, what provision will be made and who manages, monitors and reviews this provision. Priorities may change and, depending on how flexible the system, resources be reallocated. Resources are finite, however large or small, so decisions about priorities are essential. If resources are tied up with individuals in an inflexible way they cannot easily be reallocated when need arises. Resources tied into statements of SEN remain static and flexibility is lost. This argument might be extended to the debates about special school provision. The status quo is difficult to change. Is this yet another dilemma?

Responsibilities, roles and referrals

Process, policy and provision need management, monitoring and reviewing. This in turn leads to decisions about who, within the school or other organisation, will take responsibilities for the different actions and communications necessary to make this work. This is usually done by defining roles for those within the system and dividing responsibilities according to role; all within the resources of time and expertise or competence available. A school policy for SEN must be explicit about these roles and responsibilities.

In schools, SEN policy-making is about defining roles, responsibilities and referrals. Referrals depend on good record-keeping and communication systems.

Some of these communication systems are on paper, but some others happen through meetings, conferences or during training sessions for staff.

When one part of a system has come to the end of its resources of time or competence, it typically refers the problem on to another part of the organisation or to outside agencies. This referral system is part of the special educational needs policy management.

Schools as systems

Schools can be defined as open systems, which include parents and communities as part of that system. Some schools can include more of their community within the school than others. This depends on the knowledge, competence and confidence of staff and on effective policies of support and communication. It also depends on the value-system of the governors and senior management team and how these pervade the whole school.

A policy for SEN

It is said that a school that is effective for pupils with SEN is usually effective for all pupils. Such a school will support staff and parents' needs as well as pupils'. It will run efficiently and standards and expectations will be high. Such a school is likely to have a more inclusive policy for pupils with problems and differences.

Does such a school need a specific policy for SEN? The answer is definitely *'yes'* because of the decision-making processes needed to deal with the prioritisation of roles and resources. Policies are required to ensure fairness for everyone and to define roles and responsibilities and referrals. Schools' responsibility for special educational needs has increased since the Education Act 1993 and the Code of Practice 1994.

Circular 6/94 in Regulations 5 & 2(1) require schools to publish a policy document and to report on its success annually. Each school must name their special educational needs co-ordinator (SENCO) as part of this information. The roles and responsibilities of this teacher are considerable and varied. This role is itself the most recent dilemma of special educational needs. How much can or should one person do? Clearly for a whole-school approach to work, the co-ordinator must help to manage aspects of the SEN policy, but all staff will have their part to play.

Summary of Issues from the Code of Practice

For the SENCO the key issues will be:

- Has the school identified *all* pupils who may have SEN and begun to collect information about them from parents, teachers and the child him or herself? These children's names will be put on the school's SEN register, initially at Stage 1.
- Have all records and actions about pupils on the SEN register been regularly (at least twice yearly) *reviewed* with parents' views and roles recorded?
- Has the school a published policy for SEN with targets and criteria to evaluate their success in the annual report to parents?

Many schools will have a lot of planning to do in order to fulfil these requirements. Parents have a lot to offer in the planning for their own child's individual education plan (IEP), from Stage 2 onwards, because where parents are involved, progress is usually much better. Increased parental involvement in school policy-making might also be one target for a school's SEN policy.

So what are the legacies from the past that have affected our thinking? Looking back over the history of SEN may help staff reflect on their own attitudes and the value system of their school. Here are some questions to ask and discuss with colleagues:

- How has the labelling of SEN changed in the whole century?
- How has power in decision-making changed?
- How have parent and pupil rights changed?
- What effect have these changes made to ordinary schools and their policies and practices?
- How has history and past legislation shaped thinking about SEN decisions and dilemmas?

This book aims to support SEN co-ordinators in defining and developing their roles. Its audience is the co-ordinator and the head teacher, but governors, staff and parents may find it a useful source. The book examines the key aspects of whole-school SEN policy development. Each school will need to make its own decisions about the SEN dilemmas and how to resolve them in relation to local priorities and resources.

CHAPTER 2

Roles and Responsibilities for Special Educational Needs within a Whole-school Policy

This chapter introduces the theme of roles and responsibilities in mainstream schools, in relation to pupils with special educational needs. The overall responsibilities lie with the governors and head teacher. All teachers have a responsibility for those pupils in their classes with special educational needs, and parents, pupils and ancillary staff have their roles to play. The co-ordination of the day-to-day policy and practice for SEN is the responsibility of the special educational needs co-ordinator (SENCO). The fact that everyone has a role to play means it is necessary to have a whole school approach to the management of SEN.

Effective schools manage special educational needs by being clear about their priorities when allocating roles and responsibilities. Effective school policies also depend on good communication systems between all those holding these responsibilities. The school moves forward in its development by integrating special needs policies into the school development as a whole. Often what is good practice for SEN is good practice for all. Effective schools remain so by being reflective organisations which manage change. This requires a mixture of flexibility and consistency. The challenge of SEN is that of constant change and the need to adapt not only to the demands of the children but also to new legislation or resource constraints.

The Code of Practice (Part 2) describes the roles and responsibilities for SEN in a mainstream school. The duties of the governing body are given in Section 161 of the Education Act (see Appendix 2a). All must have regard to the Code of Practice when carrying out their duties towards pupils with SEN. The respective duties of all those concerned are summarised in Par 2:7 (see p.16)

Roles and responsibilities in mainstream schools

> Provision for pupils with special educational needs is a matter for the school as a whole. In addition to the governing body, the whole school's head teacher, SEN co-ordinator or team, and all other members of staff have important responsibilities. In practice the division of responsibility is a matter for individual schools, to be decided in the light of a school's circumstances and size, priorities and ethos. But schools should bear in mind the following:
>
> - the **governing body** should, in co-operation with the head teacher, determine the school's general policy and approach to provision for children with special educational needs, establish the appropriate staffing and funding arrangements and maintain a general oversight of the school's work.
>
> - the **governing body** may appoint a committee to take a particular interest in and closely monitor the school's work on behalf of children with special educational needs.
>
> - the **head teacher** has responsibility for the day-to-day management of all aspects of the school's work, including provision for children with special educational needs. He or she will keep the governing body fully informed. At the same time, the head teacher will work closely with the school's SEN co-ordinator or team.
>
> - the **SEN co-ordinator or team**, working closely with their fellow teachers, has responsibility for the day-to-day operation of the school's SEN policy and for co-ordinating provision for pupils with special educational needs, particularly at stages 2 and 3.
>
> - all **teaching and non-teaching staff** should be involved in the development of the school's procedures for identifying, assessing and making provision for pupils with special educational needs. (Code of Practice Par 2.7)

Whatever arrangements are made in a particular school, statutory duties remain with the governing body. The Code of Practice uses the term 'responsible person'. This is usually the head teacher, but may be a governor, often the chair, unless the governing body have designated another governor.

The responsible person (head teacher or appropriate governor) must, when informed by the LEA that a pupil has special educational needs, let *all* in the school who teach this pupil know of these needs and how they are to be met.

The role of the Special Educational Needs Co-ordinator

> Schools must state the name of the person responsible for co-ordinating provision for children with SEN. Parents and external agencies will then have a ready point of reference to whom to address enquiries. This may be the head teacher or deputy, the SEN co-ordinator or the head of the SEN or learning support team. (Circular 6/94 Par 31)

Under Section 161 of the 1993 Education Act, the governing body of a maintained mainstream school must report annually to parents on their policy for pupils with special educational needs. The details of what information must be included are given in the 17 points listed in the Schedule 1 (Reg. 2(1)) (see Appendix 2b) and explained more fully by Circular 6/94. Governors must also be able to show how resources for SEN have been allocated to and amongst children with special educational needs. (Circular 6/94 Par 40–42)

SEN provision

The policy must explain the school's objectives in making provision for pupils with SEN and a description of how the governing body's SEN policy will contribute towards meeting these objectives. (Circular 6/94 Par 30)

It must describe any specialist teaching expertise or units which the school includes in its provision and any specific facilities which increase or assist access to the school for those who are disabled. (Circular 6/94 Par 36/37)

Any admission arrangements for pupils with SEN who do not have a statement, must be described in so far as they differ from the arrangements for other pupils. (Circular 6/94 Par 34/35).

Integration arrangements: Schedule 1:10

> Under section 161(4) of the 1993 Act, governing bodies must ensure that pupils with special educational needs join in the activities of the school together with pupils who do not have special educational needs. This duty applies in so far as it is reasonably practical and compatible with the pupil receiving the necessary special educational provision, the efficient education of the other children in the school and the efficient use of resources. (Code of Practice Par 2.6)

Governors or head teachers might be led to think that a school's SEN co-ordinator could look after all aspects of the school's special needs practice. However, this is not a feasible option in any but very small schools, where the role may be held by the head teacher. Special needs is too broad and too pervasive of the curriculum and ethos of a school to be any one person's sole responsibility. The Code also advises that:

> Governing bodies and head teachers may need to give careful thought to the SEN co-ordinator's timetable in the light of this Code and the context of resources available to the school. (Code of Practice Par 2.8)

The development of the SEN co-ordinator's role

To understand how schools have arrived where they are today and how the role of the SEN co-ordinator has developed, it is necessary to look back over the history of the last twelve or so years.

Up to 1983, when the 1981 Act was implemented, schools did not, on the whole, consider children with *significant* learning difficulties to be their responsibility. Schools had remedial departments for slower learners or support for poor readers. They may have had a unit attached to the school for a group of pupils with a particular disability or problem. They may have had one or two children with exceptional needs that required extra advice from visiting professionals. There was barely a need for a policy for special needs, because it was thought that the great majority of children whose needs were exceptional were in special schools.

The role of the SEN co-ordinator and the concept of a whole-school policy for special educational needs has been developed over the years between 1983, when the first special educational needs training grant was offered to LEAs, and 1994 when the Code of Practice was published. It is significant that those who drafted the Code of Practice could safely assume that the term SEN co-ordinator was in such general use that it could be written into official guidance to schools offered by the Code of Practice. This is perhaps an unsung success story. All schools now accept in principle, if not yet always in practice, that they have responsibilities for special needs and that someone has to be named as their co-ordinator, even though that role may well be doubled or even trebled with other roles in the school.

SENIOS courses

In 1983 the Government offered training grants, which were for the first time earmarked for specific purposes. One of these areas was for SEN: the LEAs received a hundred per cent grant which allowed a small number of teachers from mainstream primary or secondary schools to attend a one-term course. These Special Educational Needs in Ordinary Schools (SENIOS) courses were a new concept. Their focus was the whole school, of which the course member was the representative who would develop an aspect of the schools' policy and provision for special educational needs.

Circular (3/83), and subsequent circulars, stated that the training should cover identification of special needs, extending the curriculum and access to appropriate resources. The aims of such courses were then fleshed out by consortia made up of LEA officers and tutors from Institutes of Higher Education (IHEs).

The aims of SENIOS courses was to enable ordinary primary or secondary schools (i.e. not special schools), to develop some aspect of their educational provision for children with special educational needs. The target course member was someone who had sufficient management 'clout' to effect change in their school. Early course members were heads and deputies or members of senior management. After a few years the DES used the term 'designated teacher' to describe such people. This term did not catch on. The term special needs co-ordinator (SENCO) did. However, the Code of Practice uses the term 'designated teacher' in the definition of the SENCO. (Par 2:34)

About fifteen SENIOS courses were opened across the land in the years 1984–85, in partnership with LEAs. But the original grant only covered three or so teachers in a metropolitan borough, or fifteen or so in a county area. Cowne and Norwich (1987) describe one of the largest courses of this type. But LEAs had to find ways of reaching every school and offering some substantial training and development to a least one person in each school. Some LEAs developed very useful courses in partnership with IHEs who accredited the course-work. Over the following years the amount of the grant reduced, but is still available within the current Grant for Education Support and Training (GEST) bids.

Courses aimed to increase the confidence and competence of the SENCO in areas of assessment, specialist curriculum development, resourcing and consultancy skills. A considerable body of knowledge and skill was covered by such courses.

This activity continued through the period of the Education Reform Act, with its National Curriculum entitlement and Local Management of Schools (LMS). This Act gave a new impetus to the training. Differentiation became the flavour of the month! By 1990 the role of the SENCO was firmly established and a good proportion had been trained. They did not always stay in post; many got positions of responsibility, such as deputy head or head teacher, as a result of the management training given by the courses.

Integration arrangements

As more and more SEN children with statements became integrated into the mainstream schools an additional role developed. Who would be responsible for the management of the extra teachers and assistants employed to work with the child who had a statement for special educational needs? In some LEAs a central team provided such teaching support, in others the teachers were taken on to work part-time by the school itself, either with or without a delegated budget.

Many schools ended up with extra resourcing equivalent to at least one or more of the old 'units' for special needs. The pupils concerned might have a variety of needs, not a single impairment or difficulty. In many schools the management of the extra support staff for statements became an additional role for the SENCO.

Grant maintained schools also had to work out how they would manage the additional resources allocated to cover the special educational needs of those pupils with statements. They were the 'providers' from whom the LEA 'purchased' extra support. Their SENCOs might be held responsible for allocating and being accountable for these resources. So the role has expanded and broadened in concept.

The SENCO role

The Code states that the role of SENCO is:

- the day-to-day operation of the school's SEN policy
- liaising with and advising fellow teachers
- co-ordinating provision for children with special educational needs
- maintaining the school's SEN register and overseeing the records on all pupils with special educational needs
- liaising with parents of children with special educational needs
- contributing to the in-service training of staff
- liaising with external agencies including the educational psychology service and other support agencies, medical and social services and voluntary bodies.

(Code of Practice Par 2:14)

To which could be added:

- managing statement support;
- hiring and organising other support staff;
- organising annual reviews and staged assessment reviews;
- presenting evidence for multi-professional assessments at Stage 4;
- acting as consultant to staff with pupils whose behaviour is challenging;
- reporting to governing body on SEN policy.

Time as a resource

SENCOs also teach for much of their time. Many are full-time class teachers or support teachers. There is clearly a need to select from the above list, according to time and expertise available. Of vital importance is communication between all parts of the system. SENCOs need to be part of, or in close connection to, senior management. The head needs to allocate time for liaison and planning between everyone involved. Time also needs to be allocated to see parents and give them a role in supporting their children, as part of the review process. The policy must make it clear who is responsible for each aspect of the work. Everyone needs to know the referral and information systems of their school.

There is clearly a need to relate all of these roles to resources of time and expertise available from the whole teaching staff, not from just one teacher, especially one who may well hold other responsibilities over and above those for SEN. If the role is to be manageable in larger schools, it needs to be conceptualised as more than one role, shared amongst relevant staff. These could include: head, deputy, class teacher, subject co-ordinator and year head. A time budget needs to be worked out to see what is available and to match this with a prioritised list of tasks and roles.

Activities 1 and 2 in the Activity pack give ideas for staff development exercises on this theme.

Developing and maintaining a whole-school approach

Developing these roles and co-ordinating the whole-school approach takes time. Schools are at different stages of development in achieving this. It is important, as a first step, to evaluate what your school has achieved. To do this, begin by taking an 'audit' of how staff perceive the tasks and roles which might be necessary. Who will take responsibility? who will take the action? who needs or gives information? (see **Activity 1, p.104**).

The next step of the 'audit' may be to check staff understanding and knowledge of your existing school SEN Policy. Evaluate what each believes

- *should* be the policy
- is actually the case for at present (see **Activity 2, p.106**).

Schools may well have policies on paper, but it is the improvement of SEN pupil learning over time that will be the acid test. Do the policies, for example, lead to good record-keeping, open communication between school and parents and effective use of support? Policy means intended action. But it is based on a value system which may mean changing the attitudes of some or all staff, and such change takes time. The SENCO may be a catalyst for change. But it is unlikely that change can be expected without the full support of the head teacher. A year from the start, the policy will need to be evaluated again against the success criteria of the previous year (see Figure 2.1).

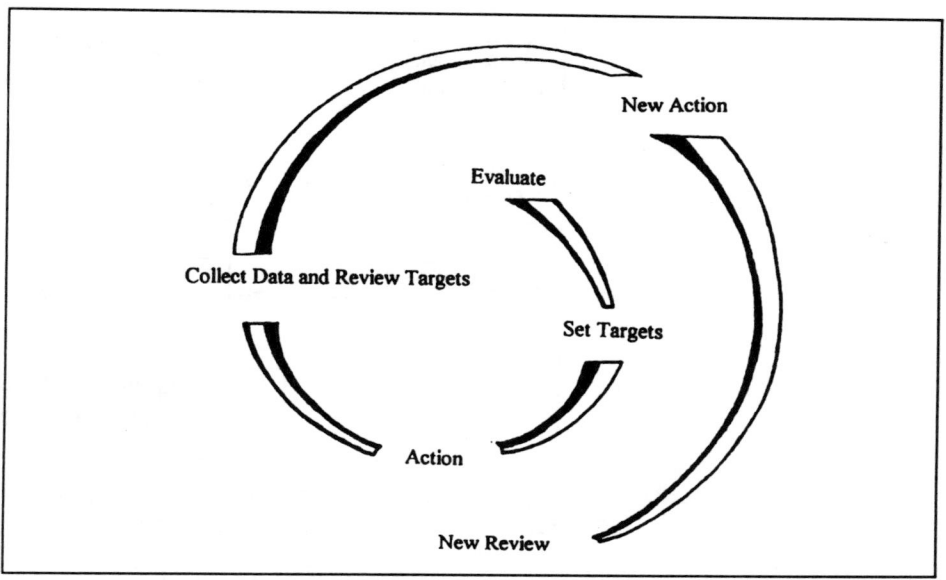

Figure 2.1: The Policy Review Cycle

Keeping the policy active Policies are like the Forth Bridge, always needing to be 'painted again'. In the first year of development, the policy is worked on by the staff and is written down. It must not just be filed, but remain active in practice.

This means that at the end of each year the policy must be evaluated.

- Were the previous year's targets reached?
- Have changes to provision or policy been made?
- Have any roles and responsibilities changed significantly or new people been appointed?
- Has the LEA policy changed in any way which will influence school policy?
- Is there a clear budget head for SEN which shows how funds from both general and specific sources are used?

These successes and changes must be made known to the governing body by the head teacher, and the governors must include this information in their annual report to parents. If the policy is to remain active and dynamic, it must be seen as a *process* of development. This requires maximum involvement of the head teacher and senior management team, representation from the curriculum and pastoral systems, as well as the co-ordination of practice by the SENCO. If effective, the whole school policy is likely to enhance the teaching and learning and well-being of all pupils. The SEN policy needs to be seen as part of the school's development plan and to link with other existing policies such as those for equal opportunities and behaviour. There should also be a strong relationship to the assessment policy and to curriculum planning (see Figure 2.2).

The following chapters of this book will cover the various aspects of a whole-school policy for SEN in more detail. Each should offer ideas for the SENCO and for staff development. Chapters 3 and 8 cover identification and assessment

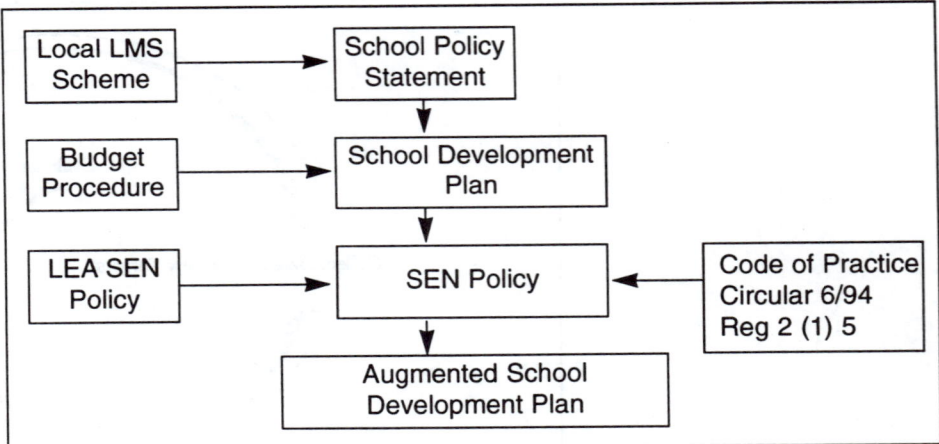

Figure 2.2: The Augmented School Development Plan (adapted from NAHT Guideline No. 2 1995 on the Code of Practice)

procedures, IEPs and reviews of all stages of the Code of Practice. Chapters 4 and 5 cover curriculum issues. Chapter 6 returns to the theme of roles and responsibilities and looks at issues related to the effective management of support systems. Chapters 7 and 9 are concerned with SENCO's work with others beyond the school, and with parents, pupils and staff within the school.

> Regulation 5, Schedule 4 states very clearly that governors must report on:
>
> 1. The success of the governing body's special educational needs policies in the period since the last annual report.
> 2. Significant changes in the governing body's policy on pupils with special educational needs since the last annual report.
> 3. The outcome of any consultation carried out under section 161(3) of the Education Act 1993.
> 4. How resources have been allocated to and amongst pupils with special educational needs since the last annual report.

IEPs — stage 2, 3 upwards

CHAPTER 3

Identification and Intervention: the Individual Education Plan

The starting point of all work in SEN is identification of pupils who may have learning difficulties of a significant nature. SENCOs have the responsibility of maintaining the school's register of pupils with SEN. Once a pupil has been identified, information gathering and assessment takes place and these contribute to a planned intervention aimed at reducing the pupil's learning difficulties. SENCOs have a major role in advising and supporting staff over such planning. For pupils on all but the first stage of the Code of Practice assessment procedures, the planning of the intervention contributes to an individual education plan (IEP) (see Appendix 3a).

The purpose of maintaining such a register and having IEPs is to improve record-keeping and planning which will make monitoring the progress of all pupils with SEN more effective. To ensure such monitoring is regular and informative, every pupil on the SEN register must have a termly review of their progress and a revision of their IEP to meet any newly identified needs. *This review process is the key to successful SEN management.*

Par 43, Circular 6/94 says that the SEN policy must explain the school's identification, assessment, monitoring and review procedures, including the staged procedures adopted by the school. Of the pupils on the SEN register, the majority will remain at Stages 1 and 2 of the staged assessment process. This means that the SEN register largely contains names of pupils who fall within the 18 per cent of SEN who have always been in school populations and have always had their needs met in this setting. Gipps *et al* (1987) describes initiatives which typical schools and LEAs had in place for this 'remedial group' before 1981. The register will also include the names of pupils with statements for SEN for whom the school is responsible.

Decisions about the SEN register

The first step in the management of SEN is to make decisions about which children will be described as having sufficient need to be placed on the SEN register. All children have individual needs, but these are not necessarily related to learning difficulties or disabilities as defined by the 1981 or 1993 Acts. To warrant a description of SEN a child should have learning difficulties that are causing concern over time, probably to both parents and teachers. Such a child is not responding to the curriculum on offer as expected or cannot cope within the normal classroom environment without additional help.

However, the Code of Practice encourages all class teachers to register any of their concerns, or those of parents, by placing the child on Stage 1 of the staged assessment process. Particular decisions seem to be difficult to make.

Bilingual learners

Children whose mother tongue is not English may still be developing their bilingual ability. At the early stages of this process, access to the curriculum as delivered is difficult. These children do not necessarily have learning difficulties, indeed they may be very efficient learners. If bilingual learners are at the early stages of learning English they should *not* be placed on the SEN register. Hall (1995) writes

> Some pupils whose first language is not English will need support to extend their speaking and writing repertoires and to practice new words and phrases in a relevant context. Schools must however ensure that lack of English proficiency is not assumed to indicate SEN or learning difficulties.
>
> p.78

There are of course some bilingual learners who do have other learning difficulties for a variety of reasons. These should not be overlooked. Discussion with a teacher from a bilingual service will be the best support where such decisions are difficult.

Speaking to the child's parents is advisable in order to understand their perception of the child's progress. It will be important to find out how long the child has been learning English and how the child functions using the mother tongue. It may be possible to arrange assessment in the child's own language through local services. Pupils should be encouraged to use their own language as well as English (see Appendix 3b for checklist).

Able pupils

Able or gifted pupils need a differentiated curriculum. They also need identification and their needs should be met by giving opportunities for extension, problem-solving and a challenging delivery of the curriculum. Schools should have a separate policy for able and gifted pupils, and curriculum planning that takes account of such pupils. They do *not*, however, have learning difficulties and should not be placed on the SEN register. Again, there may be gifted children who have other problems or disabilities. In these cases there will be other reasons for placing them on the SEN register for monitoring and further assessment. This is particularly the case when performance changes and is not what was previously expected.

George (1992) states that some gifted children show themselves as very able by their high energy level and intense curiosity, others are more difficult to spot and deliberately hide their talents. He offers useful suggestions for identification in his book, *The Challenge of the Able Child*.

Collating information about the child at Stage 1

Stage 1 allows information about concerns to be collected and collated. Parents' views and the child's own perception, as well as evidence from previous records, are included in this collection of concerns. Observation of the child within the class situation may reveal contextual reasons for the difficulty. It is important not to adopt a totally within-child model of SEN. Needs can be made by schools. The different contexts of home and school can cause conflict. Relationships within school need to be examined: between child and teacher and child and other children (see Figure 3.1).

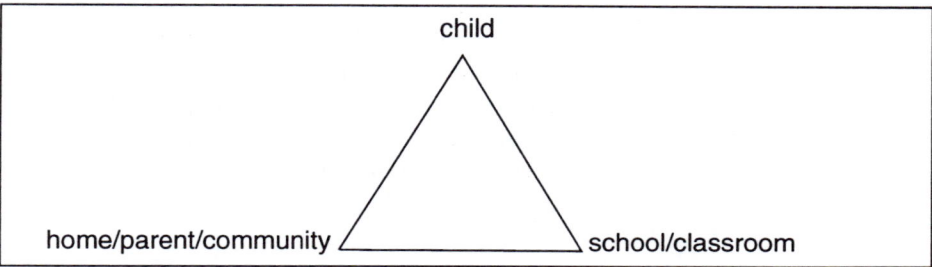

Figure 3.1: An Interactive model of Special Educational Needs

The majority of pupils can have their needs met at Stage 1 of the process of assessment. Schools now carry out a great deal of assessment within the National Curriculum arrangements. The programmes of study help teachers to structure their teaching by progression through a planned curriculum. This has both advantages and disadvantages for SEN that will be further explored in Chapter 4. The main thrust of Stage 1 is to register concerns and collect information and monitor what is happening to the child. (These can be noted on a record of concern form such as that in Appendix 3a). The next step is to carry out any further assessments which seem necessary to answer questions raised by this initial investigation. A problem-solving method is then set up (see Figure 3.2).

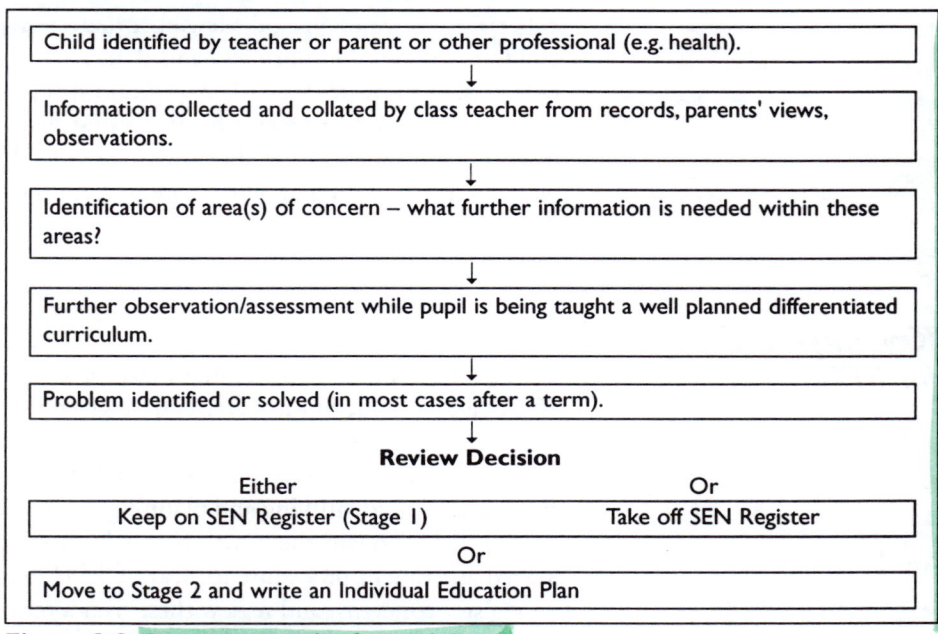

Figure 3.2: Decision chart for Stages 1 & 2

Assessment: tools and testing

The Task Group for Assessment and Testing, when planning the first steps of the National Curriculum assessment, said that:

> Promoting children's learning is a principal aim of schools. Assessment lies at the heart of this process. The assessment process itself should not determine what is taught and learned. It should be the servant not the master of the curriculum. It should be an integral part of the educational process continually providing both 'feedback' and 'feed forward'.
>
> TGAT Par 3,4 (1987)

Assessment for SEN should therefore be seen as part of the school's assessment policy and not as an additional 'bolt on' process. A full survey of assessment tools and concepts is outside the scope of this book. Numerous texts are available for further reading, such as Gipps and Stobart (1990). The following section highlights certain priorities about identification and assessment that usually concern teachers at each of the Key Stages.

Early years (nursery & reception) assessment

Children thought to have SEN in the nursery and reception classes may either be identified at entry to school or their needs may emerge over time. Teachers are sometimes reluctant to use the label SEN, because normal children develop at such varying rates, and do so unevenly across different aspects of development, e.g. language, socialisation and cognitive functions. It is therefore very important to keep careful records of pupils and record any notable differences in development. The key to good identification in the early years is observation. Teachers and helpers need training in accurate observation. They also need help in keeping purposeful records. Such records could form the basis of any decisions about SEN. Outside agencies, specifically health, may have a lot to contribute to early years' assessment. Parents should be in regular dialogue with teachers. If there are concerns in the early years, adding the name to the SEN register at Stage 1, collecting information and viewing progress is *good practice*. A large number of children will develop normally and their names will then be taken off the register before they move to Stage 2. *Significant* delay in language, combined with poor social skills, should trigger a Stage 1 assessment. Any significant delay in normal milestones of physical, social or cognitive skills should also trigger Stage 1. It is also vital to keep in touch with parents and hear their views about the child's development.

Key Stage 1: Assessment for SEN

The National Curriculum assessments at Key Stage 1 are also based on teacher observation. Some are of standard tasks and form the basis of SATs at the end of Key Stage 1. Moderation exercises have given infant teachers experience in agreeing on teacher assessments. This experience has further equipped the teachers of younger children to carry out well planned teacher-based assessment. This in turn has meant that identifying and planning for the SEN of young children has become more reliable. Again there may be a reluctance on the part of teachers to use the staged assessment procedure for fear of 'labelling' children too early, but it is better to register concerns, and review these over a term or two, than to miss out on early identification and intervention.

Teacher based assessment

For the last decade, schools have been improving their curriculum planning and differentiation, taking account of individual differences. Many schools have used teacher-based, criterion-referenced assessment, as a normal method of screening for pupils with problems and planning interventions. This type of assessment watches the process of learning and notes what the child can do as a base line. This is used to plan the next steps. A further refinement of this is objective-based assessment.

The best known initiative of this type was the *Coventry Special Needs Action Programme* (*SNAP*, Ainscow & Muncey, 1981). Many LEAs used this as a 'cascade' model for training teachers to identify and plan for pupils with SEN. The 'Portage' scheme, working with parents of pre-school children with severe difficulties and disabilities, also approaches intervention through the test-teach-test cycle. Both of these approaches stem from earlier work in special schools, and the behaviourist approach of applied behaviour analysis (see Chapter 4).

The principle is to work from what the child *can already do* to the *objective* of the next priority goal. Each task in question is split into steps. This process is known as *task analysis*. A specific criterion for success must be stated in advance, as must the *conditions* under which the task will be achieved. e.g. type of resource or level of support (see **Source List 1, p.120**).

Such an approach is ideal for monitoring progress of pupils with SEN. Often just defining the objective is sufficient to solve the problem. Once teacher and child agree on the goal, in most cases success is almost instant. Observations of how the child learns will also be made during this test-teach-test cycle. What strategies are particularly successful? What learning style does the child use? What support level is required? These observations help planning an IEP for those pupils who need to move to Stage 2.

Key Stage 2: Assessment for SEN

Often the major concern of a class teacher in a junior school is a lack of progress in literacy, resulting in poor progress across the curriculum. Can they be sure they haven't missed other causes of SEN? Have they a bias towards identifying boys? Do quiet children with needs get overlooked in favour of those whose behaviour is boisterous or noisy? There are two ways commonly used to screen the pupil population in the junior years. One is to use a checklist about learning styles, attitudes and behaviours. The other is to use standardised tests of reading, spelling and maths. Teacher-based criterion-referenced assessment should also continue to play an important part in identifying effective strategies for intervention.

Checklists

To ensure good identification, checklists are useful. These note lack of achievement or poor attitudes and poor learning strategies. Such a checklist should be used to help fill in a Stage 1 record of concern, e.g. *Stott Learning Inventory*, Green and Francis (1983) (see **Source List 1, p.120**).

Tests

Published tests and diagnostic materials can be useful to an experienced user. It is very important to familiarise yourself with the test manuals to establish fitness of purpose. You should check:

- The age range the test is designed for.
- Date of publication and the population on which it was normed (i.e. is it out of date? Or inappropriate for your class?).
- Precise instructions for giving test to individuals or groups.

These are particularly important if a reliable standardised score is to be achieved (see **Source List 1, p.120**).

Diagnostic tests can be useful in sorting out baseline information for skills such as reading, spelling and mathematics. Some diagnostic tests attempt to analyse pupil differences and malfunctions in what are described as underlying internal processes e.g. auditory sequential memory. Caution needs to be taken over the overuse of information from such test programmes. These may well lack validity in helping the child acquire a real skill within a normal class environment. The purpose of all assessment must be to lead to useful planning of interventions. Some test information does not help this process.

Miscue analysis

The best assessment is often a miscue analysis. The child is given a text of about 100 words from a book, which you think is approximately correct for his/her reading ability. You ask the child to read it aloud and say you will not be helping on hard words. It is best to have a tape recorder running so that you can analyse the reading thoroughly. You should have a prepared sheet of the text on which to mark the miscues. You should encourage the child to read but don't supply the missing words unless the child is showing distress. If the text is too hard, stop the test and do it another day with a simpler text. You should mark all the misreadings, omissions, refusals and self-corrections. This will tell you about the child's reading strategies and give you an indicator of whether the text can be read independently or only with instruction. If less than 90 per cent of the words has been read correctly, the text is only being read at a frustration level and is too hard. A text that is being read at instructional level will have less than 5 per cent of the words read incorrectly or left unread. It is important not to let children read at frustration level.

Task-analysis

As described in the section on Key Stage 1, task-analysis is the alternative approach to assessment of SEN. It is the task not the pupil that is examined in designing a small-step programme. This approach too can have its drawbacks, since the narrowing of perspectives, to achieve success in a particular aspect of a skill, can make the activity meaningless within the normal classroom curriculum. (See also Chapter 4)

Checklist of questions about assessment and teaching programmes

- Will this relate to real classroom activities?
- Does this relate to long-term realistic goals?
- Is what is being tested relevant to the learner themselves and will it enhance or damage their self-esteem?
- Can this type of assessment be carried out within the time and resources of staffing available?

Another factor which must be taken into account in assessment is the total learning process of the pupil. This includes noting relationships with parents and teachers and features related to home environments. It is very important to include notes of the child's own view of their learning and the problem you think they may have. Some pupils' difficulties in learning are caused by their emotional state or by their inability to learn appropriate behaviour. Pupils may be continually off-task, sometimes disrupting others, sometimes only themselves. Such pupils often have low self-esteem and poor learning strategies.

Good record-keeping for pupils with emotional or behavioural difficulties will note:

- Information about the pupil's learning style.
- Relationships with peers and adults.
- Relevant information from parents about the pupil in the home context.
- The pupil's attitudes to learning (can they risk failure)?
- Specific incidents which illustrate the frequency or depth of the problem.

and most importantly:

- How this pupil can be helped to function more effectively within the class.

Continuity between phases: to Key Stage 3

Transfer of information between phases, especially from primary to secondary schools, is a key issue for SEN. Whose responsibility is it to a) visit the previous school; b) sift information given orally or on paper; c) disseminate information in good time for distribution to all colleagues?

Many secondary SENCOs spend a lot of each summer holiday doing paper work to prepare records for the autumn term. Should this be their job or should year tutors share the task? There is also still a tendency for teachers to say, 'Oh I don't read records, they might prejudice me against a pupil.' It cannot be stated too strongly that *the correct flow of information between phases is essential* for all pupils, but especially those with SEN. Junior or Middle schools may have kept meticulous records. In fact that may be one of the problems. They keep too much on file, and this is not useful if the teachers in the next school cannot easily pick out priority areas of need.

Previous records should indicate those most at risk, but secondary schools do not always make use of these records as a source of information. *A key role for a secondary SENCO is to collate information from primary records* and disseminate this to all who teach the pupil. For a few pupils, transfer to secondary school is particularly traumatic and pupils need extra pastoral care. This means there must be a simple procedure to register concern and to send this information to a person with responsibility who then should inform all who teach the pupil. This is usually the SENCO's task but could be the year head's.

A systems approach to identification

It is much more difficult to collate and collect new information about pupils with SEN in secondary schools. A pupil may only be causing concern in one or two subjects, or they may be finding difficulties across the curriculum and the whole school day. One system might be to have SEN representatives in each department who collate such individual records of concern. The advantage of this system is that it is more likely to result in a good differentiation and the use of appropriate resources in each department. A cross-over of such departmental information would be needed to ensure a 'whole-child approach'. This would almost certainly require the SENCO's help. Pastoral and health needs should be noted because these are likely to affect the pupil throughout the school day. Links between pastoral and curriculum systems must be planned to ensure information flows appropriately (**see Activity 5, p.116**).

All pupils on the SEN register require a summary document of their present functioning, standards of achievement and priority needs, whether health, social or educational. Without betraying confidential material, it is essential that every subject teacher has a list of basic information about SEN pupils. This should include the potential effect on the learning processes for the child in question. Some pupils will also require full IEPs, but this should be only for a manageable proportion of the total register.

Key Stage 4

New problems may arise when pupils begin their course options at Key Stage 4. It may for example, be necessary to seek assessment exam concessions. However, for the majority of pupils, placing pupils of this age on the SEN register for the first time is not necessarily a useful way to meet their needs, unless there has been a *notable* change due to medical or other causes.

Decisions and information flow concerning Stage 1

Decisions on the following points need writing into the school's policy in the identification section.

Who needs to know about Stage 1 identification?

- The SENCO: needs to know the name and basic information for the SEN register;
- The class/subject teacher: in order to differentiate teaching;
- The parent: so their views can be added to the information and their role in helping can be decided;
- The pupils: so their views are also recorded.

Who should do this?

The identification and assessment at Stage 1 are the class teacher's responsibility in primary schools. In secondary schools, form tutors might be the best person to collate information, or possibly the year head. It cannot reasonably be left solely to the SENCO.

The majority of pupils with SEN will remain at Stage 1. They may represent about 8 per cent to 12 per cent of a school population. Their needs are met by good curriculum planning and delivery, and monitoring of progress through good record-keeping. A small number of pupils however fail to make progress, despite their teacher's intervention. For these children who have extra requirements, planning is needed, in order to 'fine tune' the programme of intervention more precisely. These children move to Stage 2 of the Code of Practice. This requires a much more specialised form of planning known as an Individual Education Plan (IEP) (See flowchart Figure 3.3).

What is an Individual Education Plan?

The term 'Individual Education Plan' came from the USA but in Britain it was only introduced universally with the Code of Practice (1994). Many LEAs had for many years developed sets of proformas to establish consistency across their schools in recording the staged assessment procedures first introduced in the Warnock report. These forms have been adapted to meet some of the additional requirements of the Code of Practice. In other LEAs, schools have evolved their own ways of recording an individual's progress. The essential features of an Individual Education Plan are listed in the Code of Practice.

> An Individual Education Plan includes information about:
> - the nature of the child's learning difficulties;
> - action - the special educational provision;
>   – staff involved, including frequency of support;
>   – specific programmes/activities/materials/equipment;
> - help from parents at home;
> - targets to be achieved in a given time;
> - any pastoral care or medical requirements;
> - monitoring and assessment arrangements;
> - review arrangements and date;
>
> For Stage 3: Par 2:105 – as above but additionally:
>
> - to seek further advice from other agencies and/or
> - to draw up a new Individual Education Plan, including the involvement of support services (Code of Practice, Par 2.93, 2.105).

In the draft Code it was suggested that the IEP would be used for Stage 1. This resulted in an outcry from SENCOs, particularly from those in secondary schools. As a result, the IEP starts now at Stage 2. All Stage 1 information has been collected about concerns and these baseline assessments of the pupils will be used in the IEP. Information is also needed about the pupil's strengths and interests. This is important because it is through these strengths that positive progress will be made. Pupil's views must be sought as well as those of parents.

The IEP is causing some concern to schools and in particular, to their SENCOs. Its purpose is to have a detailed plan of action, with targets that can be understood and achieved by the pupil and his/her teachers and parents. It must be accessible to everyone as a working document which will influence differentiation. It has to be specific and achievable but must also be feasible to use in ordinary classrooms.

The applied behavioural influence through task-analysis assessment has heavily influenced the planning of many IEPs. This results in very small behavioural goals, often related to an aspect of literacy or mathematics. These are often priority areas of concern, and targets do need to be expressed in precise enough terms and have clear criteria for success. They also have to be significant enough to affect the overall progress and well being of the pupil who is working within the normal curriculum. This issue will be explored further in Chapter 4.

Checklist of key decisions about IEP writing

- Have the concerns been expressed clearly with enough information about baseline assessments? (Tests, NC information and assessment data)

- Have the pupil's strengths and interests been recorded?
- Have the pupil's views about their learning problems been noted?
- Have parents' views and their potential roles for helping been included?
- Have targets been set, with sufficient attention to relevance and reality for the pupil and teacher and criteria for success? These targets must be specific enough for it to be quite clear when they have been reached.
- Have resources of time, support and equipment been noted?
- Is the IEP document accessible to those who need it to work with the pupil?
- Have affective as well as cognitive needs been addressed?
- Have any medical or pastoral needs been noted?
- Has the review date been set?
- When the review date comes, will there be evidence of the work done?
- How will this be monitored?

When the review is carried out will the targets have been expressed in clear enough terms for achievements and progress to be measurable? Woolly target-writing will result in an inability to know whether or not they have been met. The IEP document needs to reflect both the whole child and the whole curriculum. It also needs to identify priorities for the next period of time (usually a term). What matters to the pupil? What targets do they want to reach? How can they be helped? (See Appendix 3a for sample forms and guidelines on IEPs.)

Reviewing of Individual Education Plans

It is *essential* that pupils with IEPs have regular reviews. The class teacher can review at Stage 2, as long as parents' roles and pupils' views are included. It may be much better if colleagues work together in year groups to review; one taking the questioning role and one the answering role. A planned timetable for IEP reviews is needed for every school. Time is such a scarce resource that it must be allocated formally for this process. *It is a role for senior management to both allocate and safeguard this time for reviews of IEPs.*

The SENCO will be involved in setting up the review process, acting as consultant to colleagues and helping in decision-making for those pupils for whom it is necessary to move to Stage 3. Because of the labour-intensive nature of IEP reviews, the number of pupils in a school on Stage 2 should be carefully considered (approximately 5 per cent to 10 per cent of a school's population might be at Stage 2 of the assessment procedure at any time).

Decision and information flow at Stage 2

Decisions on these questions need to be written into school policy under the section on identification procedures. Which pupils need a very specialised programme, identifying significant needs that affect their progress in one or more aspects of the curriculum? These will require an IEP and additional support from the school's own resources.

Who needs to know about Stage 2 pupils?

- The SENCO: for the registers and to help advise on and resource the interventions.
- The class or subject teacher: to differentiate effectively for these pupils.

- The year head: for information.
- The parent: their view and role in supporting the child to be recorded.
- The pupil: so they understand and agree to the targets set.

Who will ensure that time is available and the process is monitored carefully?

- The head: to make resource decisions and to inform governors.

Who will help?

The SENCO will be called on for most of the help at this stage. However, support services, specifically educational psychologists and learning support teachers, can give advice at this stage in an informal way or through in-service training. These services should be involved at the Stage 2 review where those concerned feel the pupil needs to move to Stage 3. Parents must also be involved at this decision-point in the process (see Figure 3.3).

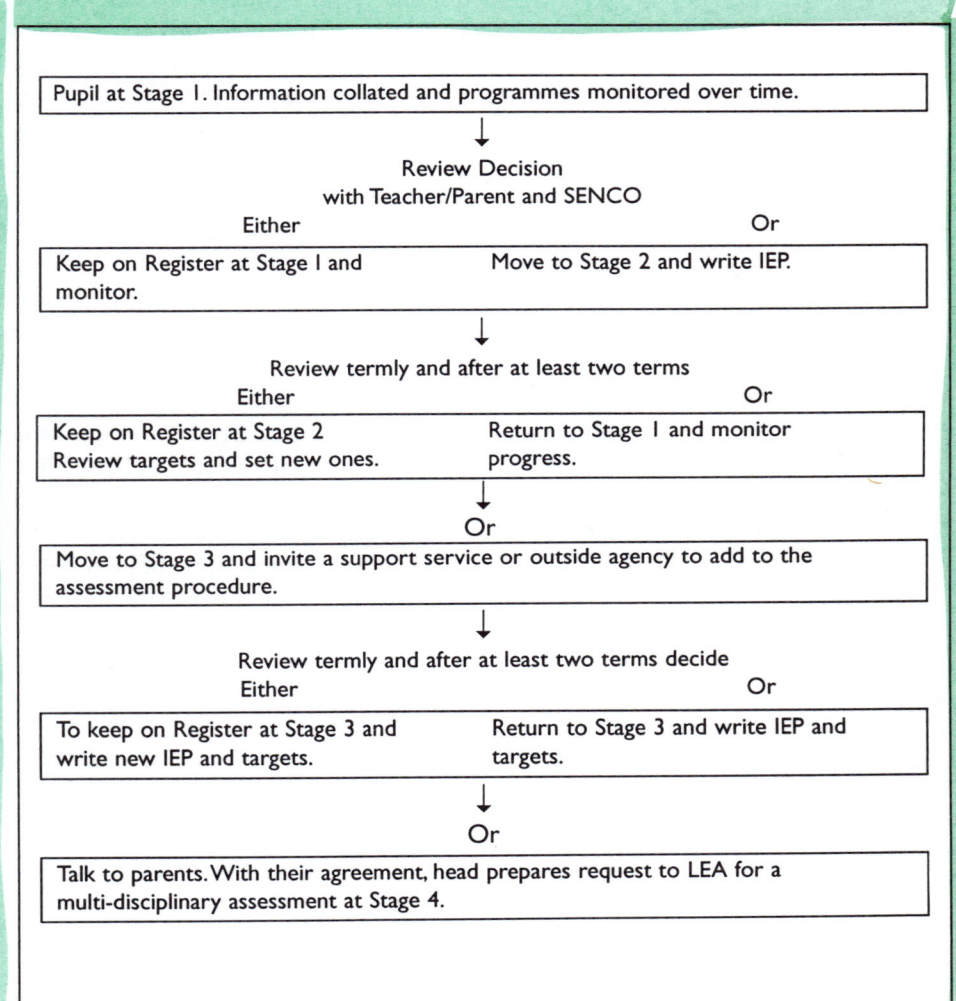

Figure 3.3 Decision chart for Stages 2–4

Stage 3

Once a pupil reaches Stage 3 of the staged assessment procedure of the Code of Practice, it is likely that a great deal of assessment will already have taken place. There will have been a working IEP for at least two terms and the pupil's learning styles and difficulties will be well known. Pupils on Stage 3 are usually causing additional concern because they are still not making expected progress. It is for this reason that outside agencies, in particular support services such as learning support teachers or educational psychologists, are called in. These professionals add to the assessment information by carrying out a range of tests or observations or by working closely with the pupil. Support services should therefore be invited to any Stage 2 review when it is thought likely that the pupil needs to move to Stage 3. It may be that, after this assessment, the advice will be to maintain the pupil at Stage 2. If the advice is to move to Stage 3, then the purpose of the outsider's involvement is to improve the IEP for the pupil. (Further discussion of working with support services at Stage 3 follows in Chapter 7.) The number of pupils at Stage 3 may be limited to the available local resources of support services. In many LEAs an audit of Stage 3 is carried out annually in order to allocate scarce resources.

It is likely that pupils will not remain on Stage 3 for ever. After a period of assessment or support they will return to Stage 2. An IEP could, however, continue to be needed for a pupil throughout their whole school life. The number of pupils on Stage 3 at any one time is not likely to be more than about 3 per cent of a school population. It could be less if the support services are in short supply. Chapter 8 continues to discuss the co-ordination of Stage 3 and beyond.

This chapter has been concerned with the majority of pupils (Warnock's 18 per cent), who remain the responsibility of the school and whose needs are met through careful assessment and planning, reviewing and readjusting targets in response to progress. This assessment and recording process is *every* teacher's responsibility, but the SENCO must keep the register and ensure the review process is carried out thoroughly. In order for this to be possible, the overall planning of time for reviews, the organisation of storage of paperwork and clear definition of roles and responsibilities, need to be part of the whole-school policy for SEN and to link to the school's assessment policy. Staff will benefit from training in writing IEPs and this again will nearly always be organised by the SENCO. (See IEP guidelines Appendix 3a). Such training needs should be identified as part of the SEN policy. The next chapter explores the term 'differentiation' and suggests various approaches that contribute to the planning of intervention programmes.

CHAPTER 4

The Curriculum: Whatever Happened to Differentiation?

The previous chapter concentrated on identifying and assessing pupils with SEN. The Code of Practice suggests this individual approach to the problems of SEN by its demands for detailed assessment and planning. This has had the effect of adding to the administrative and bureaucratic load on teachers and in particular on SENCOs. While no one would doubt that knowing more about individual children will help understand their needs, such information is only useful if action follows. The outcome of individual programming should help the pupil cope better with the demands of the curriculum and result in an increased rate of progress. The Code of Practice, however, says very little about the pedagogy required to make this happen.

The problem for class and subject teachers is that children are not taught as individuals for much of their day, but in social groupings of thirty or more. The teaching and learning process is, therefore, interactive. Within-child features play their part, but so do classroom organisation and resourcing, modes of curriculum delivery and teacher management style. Some educators such as Bruner and Vygotsky, think that learning is best conceptualised as a social process, rather than an individual one.

Gipps (1992) explains that:

> The social constructivist model of learning assumes that knowledge is built up by the child in the form of connected schemata, the child is seen as an agent of his or her own learning activity constructing knowledge.
>
> p.3

One of Vygotsky's key concepts was that of the 'zone of proximal development' (1978). This describes the gap between what the child can do alone and what they can do with someone who has more knowledge or skill. Gipps further explains that:

> Vygotsky's model suggests that not all tasks should be perfectly matched to the child's current level of development, indeed some tasks should require a shift to the next 'zone of development.' But what is crucial to this idea, is that interaction with another person

is essential, whether this person is a teacher or peer, to help this moving-on process.

p.4.

This suggests that a key role for the teacher is to build a rich learning community in the classroom. The classroom is also part of the wider community of the school and the district. It must however be remembered that influences beyond the school, local and national, affect the focus of curriculum delivery and its assessment.

The National Curriculum

The Education Reform Act (1988) and its National Curriculum is a good example of such a change of focus, which has been dictated to teachers and schools from the centre. These reforms did not originally include much about special education. The National Curriculum Council (NCC) publications later gave some suggestions, emphasising that curricular breadth should be offered to all pupils and that all teachers were responsible for those with special needs.

On the positive side, the National Curriculum gives entitlement to all children to a broad, balanced, relevant and differentiated curriculum. This means that, as Wedell (1990) says:

> the aims of education are the same for all, but the means by which the aims can be attained differ, as do the extent to which they can be achieved.

p.2

Just how the curriculum was to be differentiated was not fully explained by official documents. There were sections of the 1988 Act and its circulars to explain the possibility of exemption from the National Curriculum for pupils with SEN, or others with more temporary needs. These were not much used, as it turned out, and now the Dearing revision of 1994 removes the pressure to make formal arrangements of this type.

The School Curriculum and Assessment Authority (SCAA, 1995) now says that the flexibility of the new orders allows material to be selected, where necessary, from an earlier key stage programme of study to enable individual pupils, with or without statements for SEN, to progress and demonstrate achievement. This material should be presented within the context suitable for the pupil's age.

Organising the curriculum into subjects, programmes of study and attainment targets offers opportunities for consistency between schools. The overall content of education is now largely dictated by the National Curriculum and its assessment procedures. But as Norwich (1990b) states,

> The 1988 Act has been designed mainly for accountability purposes and this has required that its design be influenced partly by assessment and reporting considerations.

p.24

The core subjects, tested by standard assessment tasks (SATs), were likely to take over and steal time from other subjects, particularly creative activities, which could offer so much to pupils with special needs. Other problems arose for teachers attempting to fit the needs of SEN pupils into the demands of the National Curriculum. SEN pupils typically need more *time* to move through a programme of study and to master core skills and concepts.

- Certain programmes of study may seem meaningless and therefore irrelevant, to some pupils with SEN. This may be because of *lack of prerequisite skills*, or that *key concepts are unclear*, or that levels of motivation have dropped due to *feelings of low self-worth*.
- Some SEN pupils have other priority needs, which lie outside the National Curriculum. These may relate to a particular disability, e.g. mobility training for the visually impaired, or physiotherapy for pupils with physical disabilities, or needs arising from emotional trauma requiring counselling.

Modification or Differentiation?

Questions remain unanswered about modification and differentiation. Before the National Curriculum was produced, in the years after the 1981 Act, definitions of the curriculum were attempted for pupils with SEN. Three types of curriculum were proposed:

- Differentiated 'mainstream' curriculum for pupils with mild difficulties.
- Modified curriculum; probably seen as that which would be delivered in most special schools, or to pupils with learning difficulties within mainstream schools. A modification meant that part of what was on offer was in some way different from the norm i.e. possibly alternative in content, but certainly in delivery style and pace.
- Developmental; the curriculum for the developmentally young or those whose progress was particularly slow, such as pupils in schools for severe learning difficulties.

Modification is a better term to use when a different curriculum focus or a curriculum from a different stage of development is being offered for most of the pupil's day. To deliver this within a mainstream class may not be possible and may require a special class or school. Skills needed to integrate into work and adult life may become a priority, as well as those of the National Curriculum. Specialist teaching and equipment or therapies may also be needed. Such pupils usually have a statement to resource these modifications.

Modification means offering an alternative curriculum or one that is delivered at a significantly slower pace. Post Dearing, this presents less of a problem than when the 1988 Act was originally introduced. Time is now available, (up to 20 per cent of time at Key stages 1-3 and 40 per cent at Key stage 4) to be used at the discretion of the school to realise entitlement through *meaningful involvement* of all pupils in the curriculum (SCAA, 1995c). This includes preparation for the opportunities, responsibilities and experience of adult life. It could also allow time for therapy or specialist needs such as mobility training, extra tuition in reading, or speech and language work.

A developmental curriculum was one built up from small steps to meet the life skill targets or early learning objectives of those making very slow progress. A great deal of work had been done in special schools on such curricula. Research on small steps progress, in the National Curriculum, will help address the needs of this group in future (NFER 1995). Ministers have now accepted the SCAA advice that a range of provision, subject-based and unit-based, should be available to allow schools to meet the diverse needs of pupils who make progress through small steps.

But for most pupils on stages 1–3 of the Code of Practice teachers should differentiate their delivery of the curriculum. This should enable pupils, working at different levels within the key stage of the year group, to be able to progress at an appropriate rate. Differentiation is the term given to the process of planning and delivering the curriculum, teaching methods, assessment methods, resources and learning activities, to cater for the needs of individuals. According to recent advice from SCAA, this planning should be based on programmes of study and level descriptions rather than attainment targets. Whole-school planning should incorporate the modifications and differentiation required for what could be a considerable proportion of those on roll.

> Within any group of pupils there will be a wide range of ability and experience. This calls for a flexible approach allowing differentiation to provide success and challenges for them all.
>
> NCC 1989a

The IEP within Differentiation

SENCOs should not be left to deal with planning IEPs in isolation, because if they do their colleagues, delivering the curriculum, will be less effective. For the IEP to be useful to teachers and pupils, some questions will need answering:

- How will priorities and targets be jointly agreed between teacher, pupil and parent, so that all can understand what is expected?
- Should the IEP cover the whole curriculum? (It could be that a cross-curricular target is chosen; e.g. presentation of work, use of IT as access.) But how will this information be communicated to all relevant staff, particularly in secondary schools?
- Should the IEP focus on one or two small steps, related to mastery of basic skills? This may produce the best success rate and show evidence of progress, but how frequently will such targets need reviewing?

How will the IEP affect the curriculum planning for the teacher? Will the class or subject teachers have read the IEP and use the targets of individual pupils as objectives for groups within the class? This may be the most important question when writing IEPs. If the individual planning and the curriculum planning are not interrelated it is doubtful how progress for the individual child will occur. How will all of this affect classroom organisation? **The staff development Activity 3 (Activity pack, p.109)** is a useful way to find answers to these questions (see **Figure 4.1**).

Some alternative ways of thinking about interventions

The second half of this chapter looks at different ways of conceptualising interventions aimed at modifying or differentiating the curriculum. These approaches may help to focus on an individual's learning style or experiences, rather than his or her attainment level within a set content-based curriculum. The theoretical basis for these approaches and their influence on education is discussed. These approaches fall into 3 main groups:

1. Behavioural interventions;
2. Cognitive interventions, in particular, thinking skills programmes;
3. Affective interventions.

> Teachers must be very clear about the following
> - What are the core curriculum objectives for this lesson or series of lessons? How do these relate to National Curriculum programmes of study? (These may have been selected by the year group to fit into joint topics.)
> - How will these core objectives be assessed, i.e. How will teachers know if the pupils have reached a satisfactory level of skills and understanding of key concepts? Does the assessment also need to be differentiated? Will this be recorded as part of the IEP?
>
> *Additional planning for individuals*
>
> - Have the pupils (the whole class) the prerequisite skills and knowledge of concepts to begin to reach these objectives? What are the prerequisite skills for this core objective? These need to be clearly defined.
> - Have the pupils with SEN these prerequisite skills and concepts? (Cross reference to IEPs will be most useful here.) What modification will be necessary for pupils who have not mastered these prerequisite skills or concepts? Will they need 'pre-teaching?' or a different resource to assist access to information? or a different core objective?
>
> *Further questions related to continuity,v and whole-school issues*
>
> - Additional questions can then be asked about whole-school or department planning.
>   Using this approach also helps develop cross-curricular skills and concepts. What will the pupils bring from another curriculum area that can be of use within this lesson?
> - How can a resource bank be built up which can be shared to assist in differentiation of topics? Much published material is now available, but artefacts and games etc. may need to be added.
> - How does all of this effect continuity issues and group arrangements in school?

Figure 4.1: Lesson planning for differentiation

The influence of behavioural science on SEN curriculum and pedagogy

In the last two decades special needs curriculum planning and pedagogy have been strongly influenced by behavioural theories. Based largely on applied behavioural analysis these are a development of Skinner's operant conditioning theory of learning.

Skinner believed that by manipulating the environment, you could change an organism's behaviour (Skinner, 1974). First you began by deciding on the goal to be reached and then you shaped the behaviour by a system of reinforcement of successive approximations towards that goal. The reinforcement was usually food when working with pigeons, but could be praise when working with people! Skinner argued strongly that his 'science of behaviour' could include a world view of how the environment influenced mans' behaviour and indeed his culture (Skinner, 1971). During the 1980s, educational psychologists, in particular, promoted an applied behavioural approach to the analysis of learning difficulties and their remediation. As Norwich (1990a) suggests, this may have been due to a growing dissatisfaction and lack of confidence in the validity of psychometric testing and its relationship to intervention. He further explains that:

The major case for using objectives in teaching usually rests on the effectiveness of teaching and learning. Objectives are concerned with the intended outcomes for learners as opposed to what the teacher intends to do or present to the learner. This approach is an example of a rational planning model used in many other areas of social action and management.

p.90

The point here is that the outcomes are chosen and predetermined by the teacher and the child 'shaped' towards these outcomes by the process of rewarding successive steps. This is the task analysis approach to teaching that has become firmly embedded in SEN teaching and is visible in the IEP approach of the Code of Practice.

Behavioural objectives

Behavioural objectives are small scale and can only be concerned with observable behaviours. Curriculum objectives are on a larger scale and are not confined to what is observable, although outcomes have to be measured in some way through assessment. Task-analysis concerns itself with a learner's individual steps towards the chosen goal; it has less to say about teaching methods to obtain those goals, and nothing to say about any inner processes which may apply. The principle of the task-analysis approach is that success in the small steps will make a successful learner, who can then tackle new steps. There is evidence that this does work within the confines of the chosen focus. The use of behavioural objectives in curriculum planning has been very effective in some special schools.

The task-analysis approach was used as a means of giving in-service to teachers by one LEA who wrote a programme known as SNAP (*Special Needs Action Programmes,* Ainscow and Muncey, 1981). This cascade method was aimed at all primary school teachers in that LEA. As the 1981 Act came into effect other LEAs took this up as a method of focusing teachers' attention on individual needs. Primary teachers were quite suspicious of this *objectives* approach. It did not fit well with their preferred *process led* theories of learning based on a child development approach. Confusion also grew with the term 'objective' being used in both task-analysis and curriculum planning.

Wedell's (1980) model of compensatory interaction was to influence thinking about individual needs, post 1981. There was a move away from seeing learning difficulties as all within-child. The curriculum in school and the influences from home all had a part to play. The responsibility for causing as well as curing SEN fell on teachers, who were then encouraged to look at their strategies and methods as well as within-child features. Ainscow and Tweddle, by 1988, had revised their own earlier work on objectives teaching and stated its limitations. They stated that overuse of objectives could lead to:

- Narrowing of the curriculum;
- Segregation of pupils;
- Teachers feeling inadequate;
- Pupils being passive;
- The curriculum becoming static.

Ainscow and Tweddle, p.29

As a result of working with many teachers they now felt that 'the way in which objectives should be stated and the degree that objectives relate to one another are all matters of teacher judgement.' Wedell also introduced flexibility, by encouraging teachers to negotiate with the learner about objectives and to observe the pupils' preferred learning styles.

The fear of a mechanistic and technical approach to education remains and the other problem is the sheer impossibility of working at the individual small step scale when coping with large classes and with very little help.

So how can the experience of using the behavioural approach continue to be useful to those planning the differentiated curriculum for SEN?

- Objectives thinking has led to a clearer conceptualisation of individual priorities and clearer definition of needs.
- Baseline assessment has been a useful starting point on which to build programmes.
- Goal and target setting, if carried out in partnership with the pupil and teacher, can increase self-worth and the child's responsibility for monitoring achievement. Evidence can be collected, other than formal assessment tasks, to prove achievement.
- Planning, on small steps to achieve success, has proven worthwhile with the developmentally young or where the task is skill based.
- Individual priorities and goals can feed forward to inform both curriculum planning and differentiation and help teachers think about appropriate strategies to help pupils meet their targets.

It is in the area of acquiring a range of strategies and methods that teachers continue to need most help or where answers lie outside the scope of a behavioural analysis model of differentiation. Another of the shortcomings of the behaviourist approach is that by concentrating only on what can be observed, little account is taken of inner processes of thinking and feeling. Not only does this feel sterile, it discounts huge areas of human activity and culture. Another model considers interventions which enhance thinking through planned teacher mediation.

Cognitive development and thinking skills programmes

Piaget's theories of cognitive development state that a child goes through stages; first concrete operational and then in adolescence, formal operational thinking (Inhelder and Piaget, 1958). The debate about Piaget's stages and ages lies outside the scope of the present discussion. Suffice to say that Piaget and others who extended ideas on cognitive development, (Bruner, 1968; Donaldson, 1978) had significant effects on the pedagogy of the primary 'process' curriculum. However, it is the move into formal operational thinking which is most important in secondary education and which may cause problems for those with learning difficulties.

Formal operational thinking emerges during the secondary school years. It is mediated through environmental and social interaction, but is not tied to any particular subject area. The most significant attempt to intervene and change the learning potential of young people of this age group was that of Reuven Feuerstein in the 1950s. Building on a mixture of psychometrics and theories of Piaget and Vygotsky, Feuerstein evolved a solution to the sociological problem of the new immigrants arriving in Israel. These young people were not able to take places in the traditional education system and were initially labelled as backward.

Feuerstein, a clinical psychologist, challenged both the traditional trust in IQ tests and the view that intelligence was a once and for all endowment. Feuerstein et al (1979) said that the thinking skills we need in order to learn effectively, and which are normally absorbed by children as they develop in their family and culture can, if absent, be instrumentally remedied. Feuerstein developed a theory of mediated learning experiences and a programme of structured exercises known as instrumental enrichment (IE). Based on an analysis of the cognitive functions required by learners, the IE course consists of thirteen instruments, containing between one and two dozen activities and intended to be taught at a frequency of five hours a week, for a least two years. Feuerstein wished this to be free of all traditional school subject matter. Feuerstein et al (1980) (see Appendix 4a for further information).

His work opened up a whole new field of cognitive education which spread beyond Israel to the USA, Canada, South America, Russia and some countries in Europe. In the early 80s officers from several LEAs in England visited the United States and on return agreed to train teachers and set up IE projects. Their work was evaluated by a Schools Council publication (Weller and Craft, 1983). Only one of these projects survived and they published the materials known as Somerset Thinking Skills (Blagg et al, 1988). These materials help pupils to synthesise information, analyse data, and appreciate their own strategies of thinking.

In England, cognitive intervention programmes did not remain free of subject content. Possibly this was due to pressure of time, certainly once the National Curriculum began. Those who developed programmes may also have felt that these would have more validity to teachers, pupils and the public if the results could be measured in improvements in increased attainments in subject assessments. The best researched and most successful was CASE (Cognitive Acceleration through Science), a project led by Shayer and colleagues between 1984–87.

> CASE materials were designed to address individually the schemata of formal operations and incorporate the principles ... into a set of activities whose content was overtly scientific.
>
> Adey and Shayer (1994)

This project had measurable success which lasted over time and whose effects could be seen two years later in GCSE results. In their evaluation of their project the authors emphasise the need for this type of intervention to have 'duration and density' if it is to be effective. By duration they meant that it should take place over at least a two year period.

They further comment that it is not packaged materials and activities which give a new method its power, however useful as a framework. It depends also on thorough staff development which includes knowledge of the theory of the method, demonstration of skills, followed by practice, feedback and coaching on classroom presentation. Only then will mediated learning take place which really raises standards. However, as Norwich (1990b) says:

> The point is not to advocate Instrumental Enrichment as such, but to illustrate the point that cross-curricular skills may need additional emphasis for some children with SEN.
>
> p.25

Other thinking skills programmes

Other materials and methods have been used for a number of years to enhance the pupils' ability to problem solve or argue creatively within sets of rules. The best known of these are the following.

de Bono's CoRT thinking programmes (1987)

This is intended for students of twelve plus years and introduces a set of heuristics for thinking. The complete CoRT programme consists of a set of 60 lessons with work cards and teacher notes. These creative materials are intended to encourage divergent thinking and are popular with those who use them. They may be most effective when used with older or more able pupils and when they help pupils apply the strategies learnt within the normal curriculum.

Philosophy for children

These materials were developed to teach thinking to pupils of ten years or over although Fisher (1990) says that Lipman's programme can start with children as young as six years old. The method has been adapted by using pictures and videos as stimulus and back up to written material.

Lipman's *Philosophy in the Classroom* (1980) uses stories as the starting point to develop philosophical thinking through dialogue and can foster thoughtful discussion of puzzling ideas. The teacher helps children to listen to each other, take turns in speaking, and conducts the dialogue so that children learn to follow a line of argument and express their own ideas. However, teachers need to invest time in training to use the method effectively and time to deliver the programme consistently and regularly for a series of lessons over a year. When used in this way these programmes appear to improve speaking and listening and higher order reading skills as well as moral awareness. The most useful feature of all these programmes seems to be the awareness gained of *metacognition*, that is the ability to reflect on one's own thinking processes.

The cognitive demand of materials and methods

Materials used by teachers: text books, worksheets and other written materials, make two types of demand of readers. One is cognitive, the other based on reading skills. Readability is often assessed by word length and amount of syllables, but is more usefully addressed by looking at features such as legibility, complexity of syntax, amount of specialist vocabulary and interest level. The cognitive demand of materials can be assessed using a taxonomy of knowledge.

Using Bloom's Taxonomy to evaluate learning resources

Bloom's taxonomies of cognitive and affective domains of knowledge could provide such a framework for curriculum planning and a checklist against which curriculum content can be judged for its value, balance and intellectual demand. The aim is to develop higher order thinking skills by offering able pupils, in particular, sufficient challenge. The first two levels of the taxonomy are knowledge and comprehension. Few materials or methods move beyond this to application, analysis, synthesis or evaluation – the other levels of the taxonomy. (See Appendix 4b for further information)

Lessons to be learnt from What then are the lessons that can be learnt from cognitive interventions and
cognitive interventions cognitive analysis of pedagogy? The answers may be that:

- Under-achievement may be due to a lack of suitable strategies for thinking.
- Pupils *can* be taught thinking skills if the *how* of learning is addressed as well as the *what*.
- Thinking skills can be taught through curriculum subjects for the majority of pupils.
- When pupils are taught thinking processes they gain control of their own learning and this increases motivation and self-esteem.

To do all of the above teachers will need to learn how to:

- Identify the stage of cognitive development reached by a pupil or group.
- Examine the demand of the curriculum content and materials on offer and adapt these or prepare pupils to meet the demand.
- Analyse faulty processes of thinking at input, elaboration and output phases of lessons. Understand the component parts of these processes: (see Appendix 4a).
- Mediate learning through group discussions and by direct teaching of strategies to improve thinking processes.
- Teach pupils to reflect on and vocalise their own thinking processes.
- SENCOs can help colleagues to focus their attention on thinking skills as well as the basic skills which often take up the majority of SEN intervention work. This may mean finding time for both direct and indirect ways of addressing deficiencies which are at the root of the learning difficulties.
- SENCOs may be doing most to help if they master the techniques of teaching thinking skills by further reading or training (these are, however, costly of time and money).

Affective interventions Greenhalgh (1994) argues that, 'Where the curriculum and individual experience speak to each other, empowerment of the learner takes place' (p.237). Children need help to explore their own feelings and those of others. One way to do this is to keep feelings on the agenda by using those aspects of the curriculum which show the emotions of others, explore the nature of relationships and make sense of how other people overcome obstacles. Opportunities can be given to explore affective responses to particular themes. This can produce:

> A climate of warmth and support in which self confidence and self-esteem can grow and in which pupils feel valued and able to risk making mistakes as they learn without fear of failure.
>
> (NCC, 1989a)

It is important to recognise that many aspects of the curriculum can feed children's emotional growth. The worlds of story, poetry, dance and drama, art and music have a therapeutic role to play as well as being part of the cultural entitlement for all pupils. Sometimes artistic subjects are seen as having lower prestige than subjects which represent instrumental spheres of knowledge like science. It is important that areas of understanding which have a personal character are given equal value.

It is often through the creative activities that pupils who were otherwise unremarkable, begin to shine and achieve. Once this happens, the growth in self confidence can be harnessed for their less favourite subjects. The other virtue of creative subjects or teaching methods is that they allow open-ended outcomes which are not predetermined and pupil's individual achievements can be accepted. Differentiation by outcome is the norm. These aspects of the curriculum can feed the child, enriching language and ideas, encouraging creative and problem solving responses. They come nearer to the early years experiences of play, especially when taught by enthusiastic teachers.

Hanko (1995) argues that the curriculum can help pupils understand the human condition and the part emotions play in people's lives. She comments that teachers do not always realise the full potential of the opportunities the curriculum offers to explore feelings and help pupils build their self-worth. She suggests this may in part be because:

> teachers have been side tracked into mistaking surface behaviour management for a sufficient response to behaviour problems.
>
> p.76

She adds that:

> Accounts of experiences of concern to pupils can be introduced and through discussion children can speak of their own experiences but also explore in general terms what is reflected in the literature provided. Through use of consultancy groups teachers can find ways of linking personal experience to curriculum content.

(See chapter 6 on support groups).

All of the above takes place within the social context of the classroom. Managing this environment so that it produces a positive influence on pupils' thinking, feeling and learning is *the* key skill of the teachers. The environment must be flexible enough to foster learning and support autonomy and structured enough to give security to pupils and to set boundaries. Effective classrooms set within effective schools will support all pupils, but especially those with SEN. Fundamental to all of this is a whole-school culture and ethos which values individuals and allows everyone, teachers and pupils alike, to contribute to the learning process.

Positive classroom management

For any curriculum to be delivered effectively requires a positive learning environment. This in turn requires pupils to fit in with normal classroom routines and rules and to respect the rights of others. Certain pupils with learning or emotional and behavioural difficulties present a challenge to teachers. It is outside the scope of this section to explore class discipline in depth. The important point to remember is that curriculum aims include the promotion of spiritual, moral and cultural development of all children. It follows that helping children learn how to work in a harmonious way, so that everyone is respected and valued, is part of the entitlement curriculum.

Concluding thoughts

These three sections have been included to give food for thought when planning intervention programmes or thinking of different ways of delivering the curriculum to motivate learning. Clearly most curriculum planning and development of pedagogy and resources is an issue for whole-school development. SENCOs can use their particular skills and knowledge, their depth and breadth of understanding of curriculum issues to:

- Draw attention to pupils' individual differences and abilities, including their *strengths*.
- Advise and help colleagues to develop teaching strategies for differentiation which build on the pupil's *strengths and real-word experiences*.
- Remind colleagues that for many pupils, the role of the teacher is to mediate learning so that the pupil makes connections between their previous experiences and the curriculum.
- Be consultants on what hinders and harnesses learning processes.
- Develop ways of building up resource banks including IT, software and hardware, which are well indexed and accessible.
- Help school work pro-actively to meet SEN by being a *change agent* for curriculum planning.
- Inform senior management and governors of the priority areas for SEN curriculum developments. This will help governors to decide how to share *resources between and amongst pupils with SEN*, as required by the SEN policy demands of Circular 6/94 Regulation. 1.

The next chapter gives some practical guidance about the SENCO's role in relation to differentiating each of the Key Stages of the National Curriculum.

CHAPTER 5

The Curriculum: Key Issues for Key Stages

This chapter looks at some of the characteristic features of the curriculum within each phase of education. Suggestions are made about the SENCO's role in helping colleagues plan and deliver a differentiated programme of study facilitating inclusive education for all pupils including those with SEN.

Early Years, 3–5 year olds

The main characteristic of the early years curriculum is that it is firmly based on a knowledge of children's development. Play is given a prominent place, but play which is structured to encourage intellectual, social, aesthetic and physical development (Curtis, 1986, expands this in detail). The environment of the classroom should be stimulating and encourage exploration, questioning, experimentation and problem solving. The adults, led by the teacher, set up and mediate the learning experiences of the child, often by engaging in conversation which promotes the child's use of language. Stories and rhymes extend the child's repertoire of language experience into the world of symbolic representation. Such nursery education is, however, not universally available to all children.

Because meeting the individual differences in development is part of an 'early years' teacher's skills, almost every child with SEN can be included in these classes. By the reception class, children should have a wide vocabulary, be keen to learn and to take on the challenge of beginning reading and number work. Research (Tizard and Hughes, 1984), shows that early experience at home and nursery affects the skills which children have on entering school. Impoverished experience predisposes children to have more difficulties with school subjects.

There are two main groups of SEN, typically found in nursery and reception classes. The first group includes children whose needs were identified pre-school by parents and health professionals. They may have physical or sensory impairment or be significantly delayed in all-round development. Some will have statements, or programmes already devised by advisory teachers or others such as Portage workers. (A home based early intervention programme aimed at teaching parents

47

how to teach pre-school children). All should be on the school's SEN register and reviewed frequently. The SENCO's role will be to organise and ensure staff, including NNEBs, or other non-teaching assistants (NTAs), know about any specialist programmes which must be implemented.

The second group are those whose needs emerge during the early years of schooling. Typical of this group are children with speech and language difficulties or those whose social skills are poorly developed and who find conforming to group situations very difficult. For behaviour problems, support from Educational Psychologists may be appropriate. The SENCO's role is to ensure these concerns are registered, parents and professionals consulted and early intervention programmes set up. Speech and language therapists are in short supply and usually see children outside school at clinics. Help from visiting advisory teachers for SEN may be most useful in planning curriculum interventions to enhance language development.

Key Issues for SENCOs are:

- Early identification and intervention for pupils whose needs emerge in these years. Do not be afraid to register these concerns early and to ask parents for their views.
- Training NTAs and others who work with teachers to support children with SEN.
- Using outside agencies and professionals to advise and devise specialist programmes, which can be delivered as part of an early years curriculum.
- Working with parents to establish firm partnerships as early as possible.

Key Stage 1, 5–7 years

Much of what is true of early years education continues to be true for Key Stage 1. There is the added pressure to meet the demands of the National Curriculum and in particular the demands on all infant teachers to teach literacy and numeracy.

A priority will be identifying literacy difficulties early and building in extra support through use of peer and parent partnership programmes. The Reading Recovery projects have shown how successful intervention in Year 1 can be (Clay, 1993). These schemes are expensive to resource and not available everywhere. There are lessons to be learnt from the Reading Recovery experiences, particularly those from New Zealand (Clay, 1993) where a lot of group reading takes place. By careful observation and recording of progress, this programme matches the child's literacy development more closely with what is provided. In each session, previous work is consolidated but the pupil is encouraged to read a new book as well. A structured approach is needed, one which incorporates both psycholinguistic and phonological theories of how reading is learnt. (Reason, 1990)

Children need rich experiences of literature and opportunities to talk about stories and pictures, they also need knowledge of how to decode and encode print (Reason and Boote, 1994).

> Some children will need to learn about phonology and word recognition in a structured way. What is required is an assessment of the most suitable combination of methods required by the individual pupils.
>
> Reason, 1990

The teaching of these basic skills is a characteristic of these school years. But children continue to need a stimulating, enriching experience which challenges them to ask questions, explore and think. Concepts are developed through structured play, drama, creative activities as well as through exposure to stories and poetry. Classroom organisation, effective use of groups and any adult help available, is the key to meeting individual and special needs in this age group.

Research evidence, Tizard et al (1988) and Mortimore et al (1988) all points out that often teacher expectation is too low. Children need to be challenged and stimulated. This happens best where teachers structure the day well and give the pupils some responsibility for their work.

Key Issues for SENCOs and class teachers are to:

- Ensure careful recording of literacy and numeracy progress, noting children's preferred strategies and modalities (this is on the IEP).
- Some children need language enrichment toward opportunities to talk or listen to stories and share books outside those of a reading scheme.
- Provide sufficient and varied resources to meet individual needs: books, tapes, computer software, concept keyboards etc.
- Address classroom management issues and structure of curriculum delivery. Maximise teacher and adult interaction, encourage pupil independence.
- Support positive relationships which enhance self-esteem of pupils by giving value to individual achievement and encouraging listening activities like 'circle time'.
- Remind teachers that children develop at different rates. Also remember that summer-born children are often at an earlier stage of development and need the activities for this stage to continue to be available. They may have developmental, not special needs.
- Work closely with parents, both to keep them informed but also to involve them as much as possible in the work on their children's targets, especially those related to organisation (e.g. remembering kit), but also sharing and enjoying books together.

Key Stage 2, Junior years 7–11

The demands of the curriculum increase during these years, making a child-centred approach more difficult. The characteristic of these junior years is that pupils with moderate or specific learning difficulties become more visible, along with those whose emotional and behavioural difficulties block their progress. Together these make up the majority on the SEN register. The challenge for teachers is to cover individual needs of basic skills in reading, spelling, handwriting and mathematics, while at the same time giving full access to all the other subjects and experiences. It is possible that in recent years the demands of the National Curriculum have meant teachers have not had time to meet individual needs.

The skills of reading for information need to be taught at this stage. Only giving reading practice on fiction will not give pupils the skills of skimming and scanning texts to seek for facts and answer questions. Using IT to support the curriculum is also of great importance at this stage. SEN pupils benefit enormously by having every access to well chosen computer programmes.

The Junior years have been under public scrutiny in the last ten years. The report of Alexander, Rose and Woodhead (1992) challenged the pedagogy of primary teaching. This followed earlier research such as the Galton ORACLE study (1987) and Bennett's series on classroom organisation and teaching styles (1976) and match and mismatch to tasks (1984). 1995 has seen numerous discussions on class size and how this does or does not affect standards. Although t was agreed that class size affected younger children and those with SEN, there was not recognition of class size affecting standards at Key Stage 2.

These studies suggest that the key to effective teaching in these years is in how pupils are grouped and managed within the whole class. The researchers found that teachers use whole-class teaching for a considerable proportion of the day and that group work was less in evidence.

It is in the area of classroom management strategies that teachers require most help. The tension to meet individual special needs as demanded by the IEP, while delivering a full curriculum to the rest of the class, is only likely to increase with the Code of Practice. Effective use of group work, particularly when other adults are available for support, seems one solution; increasing pupils' independence through self-organised learning another (see chapter 6).

Assessment arrangements SENCOs need to be up to date with the current assessment arrangements for the end of Key Stage 2. At the time of writing, pupils with statements or others whose needs require this may need special arrangements for Key Stage 2 tests. Permission will be needed if the pupil does not have a statement or is not in a special unit. If the test timetable needs varying, more time is allowed and papers are opened early: forms will need to be sent in advance to the LEA or to SCAA (for further information see arrangements for current year).

SENCOs and teachers can work together to:

- Find ways of improving classroom management and organisation, including effective use of support staff and productive groupwork. Offer each other support, particularly with challenging pupil behaviour.
- Maximise peer group support through well resourced group activities: teaching pupils strategies of working collaboratively and solving problems together.
- Maximise use of any available adult help to reduce group size for key activities requiring mediated learning or specific teaching of skills.
- Improve planning, using IEP information to inform differentiation, both for literacy and in other areas of the curriculum.
- Teach thinking and study skills and apply to the handling of information needed for other subject areas.
- Build up well organised resource banks of differentiated materials, including games, artefacts etc. for each of topics chosen for the National Curriculum subjects, particularly history, geography and science.
- Encourage use of appropriate IT; taped books, computer programmes and recording work on tape etc.
- Continue to work closely with parents, involving them in target setting and giving them a role in helping their child.
- Improve pupils' self-esteem and motivation to learn, by increasing their autonomy and by celebrating success.

- Continue to work closely with parents and keep them informed and ask them to contribute to their own child's IEP work.

Key Stage 3, 11–14 years

Many of the characteristics of Key Stage 2 continue to apply. New features are the scale of the organisation in secondary schools and the need to work with all curriculum areas and the pastoral system. *Communication is therefore the key issue.* This begins by communication between phases and dissemination of important information to all staff about the pupils they will teach. Staff should be given key information in time to plan before mistakes are made at the critical transfer period.

For the pupil, it is important that as curriculum pressure increases, a sense of achievement can still be maintained. Systems need organising which allow targets to be chosen with the pupil, which will offer challenge but also achieve success. This will be a key role for the SENCO. Another will be the gathering and dissemination of information about pupils with SEN, so that all staff have knowledge of pupils' targets and can build these into planning of curriculum delivery.

The SENCO, or learning support team, should ideally be available to give advice and help staff development across departments on strategies for class management, differentiation by task, resource and support. Another key role will be the organisation of support for pupils with statements, as well as those at Stage 2 or 3 of the Code of Practice. They can also encourage styles of teaching which give both flexibility and structure so that pupils develop effective learning strategies. Partnership teaching may be an effective way to share expertise between the Learning Support Staff and others.

Structures for meetings, within and between departments, will need to be worked out as part of whole-school policy. Subject departments could, for example, have a representative for SEN, who meets with the SENCO on a regular basis. Links to the pastoral system are vital so that learning support departments and year heads or tutors can communicate important information about student's needs and actions to be taken. Good practice has been developing in many secondary schools. Gilbert and Hart (1990), for example, have many practical suggestions of how whole-school policies for SEN can work out in practice. Target setting for all pupils can be linked to systems of academic tutoring aimed at raising achievement for all.

Key Issues for the Learning Support Department are:

- Collecting information from each department about individual pupil's progress and sharing relevant information with colleagues.
- Designing IEPs with pupils, so that targets are challenging and achievable and self-esteem enhanced. Reviewing these frequently.
- Organising effective support for pupils on the SEN register, particularly Stages 3 and 5 (see chapter 6).
- Dissemination of SEN information amongst relevant staff and departments, including special assessment arrangements at end of Key Stage 3.
- Supporting curriculum development and differentiation, practically with ideas and resources. Encouraging the teaching of study skills and checking on readability of texts and worksheets.

- Informing senior management of time and resources needed between and amongst pupils with SEN – *(A key issue in the SEN policy).*
- Continue to work closely with parents, keeping them informed and listening to problems. Some of these arise round homework. This can be difficult for SEN pupils. The SENCO may need to mediate between subject teacher and pupil to make homework demands reasonable for the family and pupil.
- At the end of Key Stage 3 ensuring that students have access to careers guidance working in partnership with career staff or services.

Key Stage 4

At Key Stage 4 the issue about differentiation or modification changes to one about choice of courses and subjects. The subject is confusing. Greenhalgh writes:

> In the attempt to establish a national qualification framework based on the academic, vocational (GNVQ) and occupational (NVQ) routes within Key Stage 4, some of the student-friendly courses such as the diploma for vocational education are under threat. At a national level consideration is being given to developing coherent accredited stepping stones onto a national qualification framework. But these have not yet been clarified and in the meanwhile the market is confused about the relative value of a variety of other accreditations e.g. new GCSE short courses, AEB basic tests; Skillpower, Number power, Duke of Edinburgh Awards, accrediting core skills, etc.
>
> Greenhalgh (1995)

SENCOs have an important role to play within the school's decision-making about what courses should be on offer. With their knowledge of student perspectives gained through negotiation of IEPs at Key Stage 3, they will know much about the aspirations and capabilities of students on the SEN register. This knowledge can influence the school's policy and planning about how option choices are put together.

For pupils with a variety of SEN the types of course taken and the method of assessment related to the different kinds of course will be of vital importance. The overall load of the curriculum at Key Stage 4 should be considered for students who may work more slowly, or may have difficulties in communication either orally or on paper.

Special exam arrangements

SEN students may require special arrangements in examinations at sixteen. These are additional provisions on circumstances permitted during coursework assessment and terminal exams. They apply to those students whose SENs have implications for the way they need to be assessed. With external exams at Key Stage 4 it is important that the examining body knows a pupil's assessment needs in advance. The school must prepare special information to demonstrate the pupil's SEN and related assessment needs. (SCAA 1995)

This may well be a cross-curricula issue and will need co-ordination. Subject staff will need to know about the types of arrangement possible and about student needs. It is most likely that the SENCO will have an important role in helping the school and departments with in-service for this, followed by co-ordination of paperwork for the students in question.

The post-Dearing revision of the National Curriculum still emphasises the right to entitlement and access for pupils with SEN. At Key Stage 4 this may include using the freed up time of 40 per cent to provide opportunities to develop life-skills for independent living, or for the move to college. This in turn may mean cutting down the number of subjects taken at GCSE or considering alternative forms of accreditation. It is important that pupils leave school with some form of accreditation which reflects their abilities and interests and achievements. It is also important that students are encouraged to take responsibility for their own learning. This is much more likely if the course on offer matches the students' own requirements and interests. Teachers argue that a Records of Achievement approach could be supplemented with formal external accreditation arrangements. Short GCSE courses, GNVQ courses and courses accredited by other organisations such as RSA and City & Guilds are all being considered by schools. A full discussion of all that is on offer lies outside the scope of this book. SCAA regularly publishes documents on Key Stage 4 and SENCOs need to keep up to date with the current situation, which is changing rapidly at present.

The key roles and issues for the Learning Support Department at KS4 would seem to be:

- Continuing to talk and listen to students about their priorities and aspirations.
- Helping students to self-regulate and monitor their own progress.
- Helping colleagues to recognise the students' strengths and not to emphasise weaknesses.
- Finding ways to demonstrate these strengths by choosing suitable accredited courses.
- Co-ordination information which will contribute to transition plans for those with statements.
- Providing information about courses on offer to students and their parents available both in school and at local FE colleges.
- Helping colleagues understand the special arrangements for exams that may be available and needed for SEN students.
- Helping to prepare information to accrediting bodies about students special examination arrangements.

Much of this requires whole-school planning and is, as SCAA suggests, for school staff, governors and parents to discuss in order to determine the purposes, principles and possibilities surrounding Key Stage 4 choices. The SENCO has a vital role in bringing the SEN perspective to these vitally important discussions.

Summary

The last two chapters have looked at different aspects and models of differentiation. Curriculum arrangements are part of a school's development plan. This will need to link to the school's SEN policy (see Chapter 2). SENCOs have a key role to play in helping integrate these two policies.

Differentiation had become a 'buzz' word in the period after the passing of the Education Reform Act. By now the principle should be embedded in practice, as seen by OFSTED inspectors in their evaluation of lessons. Teachers however, still need help in clarifying what the term means for them within their class or their subject.

Differentiation is clearly about planning and organising tasks, resources, support and it is about differentiating assessment modes or levels and getting feedback to the student about progress. But it is also about establishing learner-centred methods of delivery across the curriculum boundaries. The pupil increasingly should take control and learn to negotiate their own targets, take risks, work with others on open-ended as well as prescribed tasks. Individual Education Plans need to feed into the differentiation planning. Ideally, if this planning were perfectly done for every pupil, there would not need to be special needs paperwork which was seen as a separate system of recording. But if the IEP is to be effective it has to be flexible and incorporate different ways of conceptualising target setting.

For some skill based areas of learning, an objectives approach using small steps, is most effective (see section in Chapter 4). But for other areas of learning a more open-ended approach will be needed. As Norwich suggests:

> a broad and flexible attitude needs to be developed as to what is a target, in an IEP. Targets may be written as:
>
> - Specific objectives in observable learner outcome terms for which specific teaching strategies can be derived.
> - Sets of related and more general objectives linked to general teaching procedures, or
> - Learning outcomes based on general teaching principles with expected outcomes of only the most general kind.
>
> Norwich (1995) p.29

Earlier in this same discussion paper, Norwich debates the idea that some areas and levels of learning cannot be isolated from each other and broken down into small detached linear steps. As was discussed in this book in Chapter 4, alternative models may be needed which include a focus on creative and original outcomes, whether in cognitive or artistic areas of the curriculum.

As Norwich concludes, 'this model calls for identifying learning encounters or processes without any specific preconceived ideas about outcomes. He adds, '*the position taken on these issues will influence how you approach drawing up IEPs.*'

It will also influence how schools develop their future curriculum particularly as flexibility has been introduced through the new National Curriculum arrangements.

CHAPTER 6

Managing Effective Support

In recent years, one of the roles which has expanded for SENCOs or senior staff, is the organisation and management of support systems in schools. Additional staff may have been allocated by the LEA for pupils with statements. These could be teachers or non teaching assistants (NTAs). Pupils on Stages 2 and 3 of the Code of Practice may be offered support from the school's own resources, or at Stage 3, from visiting teachers. All of this needs co-ordination and management. Extra staff joining the school should have clear job descriptions, induction and guidelines about school procedures and practices. New staff allocated to a support role for the first time will also need training. The SENCO's role in relation to the co-ordination and management of support could be significant. It could include the need to:

- Establish the support needs of pupils and colleagues.
- Arrange and monitor support timetables.
- In conjunction with senior management team, hire, induct and manage support teams.
- Arrange liaison time for support teams and subject teachers, including liaison time with the SENCO themselves.
- Provide support personally to pupils or staff.
- Organise staff development for support teams.
- Build links with outside support services and agencies and liaise with them to ensure good partnership can occur.
- Support individual parents through interviews and case conferences.
- Keep the senior management team and governors informed over support issues and resource implications.

This description seems daunting, but is based on observation of the work of many SENCOs. It becomes clear that in large schools, or those with many support staff, the management of support requires time and expertise to be carried out effectively. Mortimore's (1994) recent study of associate staff examined the management and cost effectiveness of employing a range of people for support and administrative roles in schools. These authors discuss the issues which arose from their research, which include:

- Appointment procedures.
- Contracts, job descriptions and pay scales.
- Communication between post holders and line-managers.
- Training and appraisal.
- Exploitation.
- Boundaries with teaching staff.
- Benefits to the school and pupils.

Much of this lies outside the scope of this chapter but these issues should be given some thought by senior managers and governors when employing extra staff. What this chapter will attempt is to explore how to use classroom support most effectively. The answers suggested come from a variety of sources.

What is effective support?

What is considered to be effective support and for whom?
- Support for the child?
- Support for the curriculum?
- Support for the teachers?
- Support for the family?

To this one could add support for the SENCO!

Support for the child

Pupils with or without statements will have IEPs which set targets (as explained in Chapters 3 and 8). Part of the strategy to meet these targets may be to offer additional support from an adult, a teacher, NTA or occasionally a volunteer parent. This adult works alongside the child in class. Their role is to help the pupil be as independent a learner as possible. So they will check that instructions have been understood, keep the pupil on task by encouragement and praise, as well as adding additional teaching points. This type of support is often given by NTAs and is particularly productive for younger pupils.

An additional teacher should be expected to do more than this. They should be helping plan the IEP for the child and be teaching certain aspects directly. Sometimes, for very short periods, this extra teaching takes place outside the classroom in a withdrawal group. The pupil must not miss out on the curriculum on offer, so such sessions must be carefully planned to back up what is happening in class. For basic skills programmes of reading, spelling and mathematics, such withdrawal support can be effective. Small group work within class may be just as effective although this depends on features of classroom organisation and space. In some rooms finding space for extra adults is a problem. There just isn't room! For certain activities, especially those requiring careful listening, the class environment is too noisy. In other cases the group activity itself will be too disruptive to the rest of the class.

A lot has been said about the effects of withdrawal support on the pupil's self image. Younger pupils rarely mind being taken from a group because their need for extra attention is so great. With older pupils, it may be best to negotiate with the pupil and let them choose what sort of support they would like. Often a 'clinic' approach for such difficulties as spelling and reading can result in self-referral. After a discussion, strategies to overcome problems can be suggested and support offered.

This is particularly effective for older pupils, especially when they are preparing coursework.

Adult support is most often given to small groups, even when the target child is the one for whom it was allocated. Pupils need time and space to attempt tasks, make and learn from mistakes and develop autonomy. An over-protective type of support will suppress independence.

Whatever individual support is available, *it cannot compensate for a poorly differentiated curriculum*. If the focus is solely on the child and not the curriculum and classroom content, this form of support may fail. This is, of course, one of the dilemmas of SEN; the tension between meeting individual needs and the requirements of accessing the National Curriculum. The location for support need not be problematic, as long as what is offered meets the needs of the pupil by helping them access the full curriculum and the school's normal activities. *The task of the SENCO is to keep integration issues in the forefront of everyone's mind when planning support timetables.*

Support for the curriculum

This view of support can be seen as an additional means of ensuring that the curriculum is accessible to a wider range of pupils. It often takes the form of collaborative partnerships where both teachers plan and deliver aspects of the subject and where good use of group work is possible. It requires excellent joint planning to use the skills and knowledge of both teachers.

Hart (1991) analyses the risks and rewards of the collaborative classroom. She points out that official reports, such as that of the HMI in 1989, on support teaching, omit to state how difficult it is to achieve successful collaborations between class or subject teachers and those in support roles. For many teachers, having another adult in their classroom presents a threat to their control or a fear of criticism of their work. Even when both adults are happy to work together there are difficulties to overcome. The support teacher who is the 'outsider' may have to start by establishing their credibility. Preparing good materials and offering support with differentiation, may be a start. Once 'entry' has been accepted, then working in a flexible way to support both the curriculum, the teacher and the child or group of children will begin. Ground rules about control, beginnings and ends of lessons, marking work, need to be established.

There are no set rules, each pair or team needs to work out what is best for their own context. The best partnerships recognise the different strengths of their members, allowing control of content, delivery and assessment to be shared. Teams which include NTAs need to recognise that some tasks are not appropriate to be given to the non-teacher. Such tasks would include whole-class teaching and unsupervised group work outside the classroom. NTAs on the other hand, are very good at understanding children's emotional and social needs, preparing materials under guidance and carrying out well planned IEPs, if the strategies and targets have been explained. Secondary schools, particularly grant maintained schools, have recently increased their use of NTAs for support work to reduce cost. In such situations, it will be *even more important for the SENCO to establish policy guidelines and job descriptions for use of NTAs.*

But NTAs can support the curriculum too, perhaps not by planning whole lessons, but by sharing ideas of how to follow up a theme or produce a resource. NTAs often say they are an underused resource: 'If teachers would only explain what they want the children to do – we could prepare better and get materials together' is often what is said by NTAs in training sessions.

When the team is made up of two teachers then it is possible to change roles occasionally and the class teacher becomes the supporter and the support teacher takes the whole class. Working with an individual or small groups can then give the class teacher an opportunity to observe faulty strategies used by the pupils and to understand how better to intervene.

Liaison time

Hart (1991) says that successful collaborative partnerships are made, not born, and are a product of continual careful negotiation. The classroom context is part of the experience that affects children's individual responses to learning. These are a product of the conditioning that goes on in classrooms. Hart (1995) argues that differentiating the curriculum to meet individual needs is also about understanding these classroom processes. She says:

> What we call individual differences are thus not objective descriptions of individual qualities and characteristics which exist independently of school and classroom contexts and the interpretative frameworks of teachers. They are products of school and classroom processes not simply a natural reflection of inherent differences in children.
>
> p.38.

Working together, adults can help each other make sense of the complexity of the classroom environment. Successful teams will use time to analyse the various elements of classroom interactions and evaluate how support can best contribute to solving the various problems that arise. The problem is that time is scarce and rarely of sufficient quality to allow this to happen. Liaison time is often not seen as a priority by senior management. *It will therefore be an important part of the SENCO's role to fight for such time to be available for classroom teams to work together on some regular basis.* Without liaison time, what could be the most effective way to support the curriculum and the child with SEN is ineffective and this considerable additional resource could thus be wasted.

Support for the teacher

This may not seem very different from the support for the curriculum, but perhaps is more to do with partnering, of a different kind. It occurs most when NTAs or parents work for large parts of the day in one class or where support is otherwise available on a regular basis. Support is then seen as a resource which the teacher manages along with organisation of tasks and the physical resources of materials and space. From this point of view, the teacher is the room manager in charge of the team and as part of this managerial role, deploys the time of extra adults to particular tasks. The teacher is supported if this room management is efficient and everyone knows their role.

Thomas (1992) found that the self-selecting teams of teachers, parents and assistants that he questioned in his research relied very heavily on an 'affective schemata'. A premium was placed on positive interpersonal relationships and unspoken understandings. Teachers could find other adults in their classes stressful. Their reaction to this was to reinforce their professionalism and defend their territory. Classroom support could, in these cases, yield diminishing returns to pupils if these stress reactions were too pronounced.

However, the opportunities that are presented by routine working partnerships are tremendous. Better differentiation and group work can take place. Learning can better be mediated by an adult working with the pupils to enhance thinking and language. *SENCOs should explain to senior managers that classroom teams need time to work out their respective roles and responsibilities and a way of working together.*

The training of NTAs together with class teachers

In the last fifteen years a quiet revolution in classroom practice has been taking place. Classrooms are no longer places where you find one adult teaching a group of thirty children. Now you can find several adults working alongside the teacher in many classrooms. Since the Plowden Report (1967) parents have been seen as a valuable resource for classroom assistance in primary schools and such help has been common in many infant schools. The more recent explosion of support has come largely from the practice of employing NTAs some of whom work with pupils with statements. Most LEAs appoint such adults for a number of hours per week to work alongside the class teacher to give support.

Recently GEST funded programmes have been available to train Key Stage 1 special classroom assistants. A large number of LEAs are giving some training to NTAs supporting children with statements. Baskind and Thompson (1995) in their survey of the use of NTAs for SEN support nationally, mention training initiatives developed in Wiltshire SAINTS, (1989), Oxford OPTIS (1988), Leeds and Calderdale (see **Source List 2, p.121, for training information**). A London group of LEAs are at present sharing information about both accredited and home-grown courses they offer. But this expansion of the adult work force in schools was unplanned nationally and no national training initiative or appropriate career or pay structure has been developed as yet.

Defining the role of the NTA

Balshaw (1991) gives useful guidance on the training needs of the non-teaching assistants and offers useful activities for training within her book. She lists the basic principles which should be addressed when considering such a training programme. These include:

- Establishing clear roles and responsibilities. This includes relationships to pupils, parents and teachers.
- Gaining clear understanding of the communication systems of school and class.
- Establishing ground rules for each team – valuing the assistants' work and not using them as 'dogs bodies'.
- Making use of personal skills and strengths.

To which I would add:

- Understanding National Curriculum Key Stages and assessment procedures in outline.
- Giving some general principles about teaching reading, writing and mathematics.
- Outlining key issues about managing behaviour.
- Different types of disabilities and learning difficulties.

Personal experience of setting up training in two London boroughs has led me to realise what a valuable resource these support assistants can be to teachers. They are very keen to attend training and soak up everything on offer. The problem then arises that training assistants away from the schools may not in itself help develop good teamwork in classrooms. The teachers *also* need help in working with other adults and managing this resource effectively. This applies particularly to teachers of older pupils who may not be so used to working this way. Lorenz (1992) in a useful survey of support staff issues, emphasises the importance of involving class teachers and the difficulties of schools managing to release both at once for training.

The Audit Commission Report (1992b) has a short section on working with non-teaching assistants. In this the authors comment that they often observed assistants sitting in lessons which were entirely teacher directed, such as a story or a TV programme. They questioned this use of time as being too passive and suggest that better planning could result in a more productive use of the assistant's time. They suggest better planning for differentiation and clearer definition of the purposes of support are needed.

In my experience NTAs are very often frustrated by lack of clarity from teachers as to the curriculum goals to be reached. Pre-requisite skills and concepts can be rehearsed with pupils prior to a lesson. Specialist materials can be produced by NTAs under instruction. Innovative ideas are often thought of by assistants as long as the curriculum goals have been made clear to them in *advance* of the lesson delivery. *Allowing the full potential of all in the team for the benefit of the children, may require some joint training, including the understanding of the importance of role definition.*

Room management: an example of planning classroom support

At its best, the classroom team with an NTA and teacher working together, can bring about very effective learning for pupils with SEN and others in the class. What makes such teams effective is explored by Thomas (1992). He carried out research into both the planning and practice aspects of this partnership. He suggests that it isn't necessary to leave team building to chance by relying on good relationships worked out over time. From his research there is evidence that some agreement is needed about the potential roles of all those in a classroom at any one time. He calls such planned organisation of roles 'room management' and takes some of the ideas from excellent work done in special schools. The tension for a class teacher is to manage both the individual needs of pupils and the activity of the whole class. Splitting these roles, for any one period of time, and giving the role of 'individual helper' to one adult and 'activity manager' to the other, increases on-task behaviour of pupils. These roles can be reversed at certain times, but the change round should also be part of the planning. (see Activity 4, p.112, **for further development of this idea**).

Support for pupils with emotional or behavioural difficulties

Pupils with emotional or behavioural difficulties present a different kind of challenge when planning support. Clearly they too need access to the curriculum and help to overcome blocks to learning which arise from their internal state of anxiety or fear of risk taking. Teachers too need a different quality of support when facing challenging or worrying behaviour, establishing classroom rules and building positive relationships. A behaviour policy for the school should not only be about rules, rewards and sanctions, but cover staff development and the support needs of teachers.

Teacher support groups to help support pupils with EBD

Hanko (1995) explores in depth how staff development groups working with an outside consultant or a specially trained member of staff, can work together in a problem solving mode. Building on her work in both primary and secondary schools, developed over a number of years, she explains the purpose of such staff groups. Each session focuses on a specific child and through sharing the knowledge of the teachers present and the skills they already possess, the group helps them to find answers which will improve the situation and help the child cope better. She says that by helping teachers realise the depth of knowledge they already possess about the learning process, the curriculum and child development, their objectivity is restored and confidence gained. She suggests that knowledge can be shared about: the child, the whole classroom group in relation to the child, the teacher- pupil interaction and the therapeutic potential in the day-to-day curriculum.

The skills can be shared about:

- gauging the needs of a specific case from the behaviour displayed;
- making special bridging efforts to reach the child's 'teachable self';
- providing a consistent setting of new learning experiences likely to meet the needs gauged;
- if possible involving the child's parents and, if necessary, colleagues (fellow teachers and members of other professions) as genuine partners. (p.62)

She further suggests that by working on the underlying issues, the whole group of teachers develop problem solving skills which they can use in other cases.

The SENCO's management role versus their role as a support teacher

Many SENCOs work as a support teacher themselves for part of the week. This may be for a few lesson periods, or even a whole timetable that they can organise themselves. SENCOs are very experienced teachers and can have much to offer by way of help to pupils and their teachers. A secondary SENCO writes:

> The further you get away from the classroom the harder it is to give valid advice, so working part of the week with a *hands on experience*, keeps you up to date with materials and techniques and lends credibility when giving advice to colleagues.

However, it is important to be clear about roles. The SENCO's role is to co-ordinate the SEN work in the school. If they choose to deliver support for too much of the time this could leave too little time for their organisational and management work. Another important task is to encourage other teachers to differentiate the curriculum and organise the classroom so that the majority of needs can be met from within normal resources of the school. The SENCO will be needed most for advice for those with more intractable and persistent needs. *SENCOs have a role in helping assess pupils' needs and design and review IEPs with staff, especially at Stage 3.*

This may require them to teach in order to work this out in practice. The question which always must be kept in mind is:

- How will this activity support the teacher to support the pupil?
- Does this enskill the class teacher as well as helping the child?

SENCOs must keep an overview of what is happening to support staff in their school. This means setting up a system of meetings, where the different groups can voice concerns, sort out problems about children or staff and generally feel supported themselves.

Support for the SENCO Who supports the supporter? For an effective SEN policy to work the SENCO needs support from senior management. They should work to a deputy head or be part of the senior management team. There are many decisions which need to be shared and communication is vital between the SENCO and management.

Some LEAs have set up network meetings to support the work of SENCOs and to share ideas across the district. Such networks give everyone opportunities to hear what others do, to problem solve and to agree on local procedures and priorities. If this is not happening, perhaps a cluster of schools could get together to arrange meetings, or make themselves into a branch of a national organisation such as NASEN (National Association of Special Educational Needs) (**see Source List 3**).

Training for SENCOs Galloway (1985) and Hanko (1995) both emphasise that to meet the needs of children with learning and behavioural difficulties it is necessary to meet the needs of their teachers. To address these 'teachers' needs' requires well targeted in-service which helps staff to become more confident and competent. The SENCO is often required to take a lead in this process. This means they need training which focuses not only on knowledge but on the consultative skills required to help others. As Hanko (1995) states, 'Such skills take time to develop and it requires support to practise them in the face of the range of complexities which confront special needs co-ordinators.' (p.140)

SENCOs also need access to longer training courses. The roles and responsibilities required by SENCOs depend on their own experience, knowledge and skills. To be effective, SENCOs require *substantial training* and experience. They should be able to attend at least a one-term equivalent accredited course or build up credits towards an advanced diploma or degree. Courses are available at some Institutes of Higher Education and some GEST funding can be obtained through LEAs. It is worth making enquiries to the colleges and SEN adviser or inspector. Such courses will expand on all the issues raised in the chapters of this book. However, an important part of all training is the opportunity to meet fellow teachers and to share problems and ideas for their solutions. *Opportunities to share ideas*, learnt from training experiences, back in school with subject departments, year groups or class teachers *will also need building into the school's staff development programme.*

Support for the family This is a rarer way of conceptualising support, but in fact a lot of school SEN time is spent in just this activity. Talking to parents of children experiencing difficulties, listening and being aware of parents' anxieties, entering into agreements over goals, are all ways of supporting parents and through this, their children. This aspect of the SENCO's consultative role is explored further in Chapter 9.

Specialist support Certain pupils will have needs which cannot be met within the school's normal resources of expertise. These pupils are usually on Stage 3 or already have a statement for SEN. Such pupils will need support from visiting professionals who have specialist training and access to specialist or scarce resources, some of which they may provide or loan to the school. Such pupils include those with severe hearing impairment, visual impairment, physical impairment, or language impairment; severe literacy problems or emotional and social problems. Knowing when to ask for such help and from whom, liaising with such specialists and keying their work into the school day and to the curriculum, is another major role given to SENCOs. This will be explored further in the next chapter.

Summary

This chapter has explored in some detail types of support and considered how to make support more effective. Several points emerge for SENCOs to remember. These are:
- Teachers and other adults working together in classroom need training opportunities to develop good teamwork and communication.
- Time is required for this process across the week and the year.
- This time for liaison and training must be allocated by management as part of the school's SEN Policy.

Support staff should have job descriptions and guidance notes on induction. They also need a line manager with whom regular meetings are possible. **SENCOs have a role in explaining the importance of these issues to the senior management and governors. If not addressed, a valuable resource may be wasted or not used efficiently for the benefit of the pupils.** (See OFSTED report on *Promoting high achievement for pupils with SEN*, 1996).

CHAPTER 7

Multi-professional Networks

This chapter looks at the partnership with bodies beyond the school and how this links to the school's SEN policy and practice. The third section of Schedule 1 Regulation 2(1) (see Appendix 2b), lists these areas at points 14,16 and 17; points 13 and 15 will be covered in Chapter 9. The practical aspects of using external support services and agencies is then considered in some detail. The chapter ends with some descriptions of joint actions required by schools and agencies at key transition points for the pupil with special needs.

One of the key roles for the SENCO is that of getting to know and work with all the various support services and agencies that are available locally. Added to this, there is a need to be aware of the voluntary organisations which have national networks and local branches or representatives. These organisations provide information on specific disabilities and support parents of children who have these problems. They may be able to put parents in touch with others who have similar difficulties, to form a support network. SENCOs also should to be aware of local special schools and any link or cluster arrangements between schools that have been developed. All of these services, agencies and organisations will work with parents, as will the school. The SENCO often plays a co-ordinating role for parents by putting them in touch with the multi-professional network, or by collating information from the various agencies who may work with the child and family. Parents' roles vary, from 'key workers' for those who have for years co-ordinated information about their child, to parents who are diffident and need encouragement to share decisions with the school. The SENCO also has a key role in leading other staff and ensuring that appropriate in-service is available regarding the various aspects of SEN, including working in partnership with those beyond the school.

Use made of | Schedule 1: 14
support services

> Special educational needs support services can play an important part in helping schools identify, assess and make provision for children with special educational needs. Such services include specialist teachers of children with hearing, visual, and speech and language impairments, teachers in more general learning and behavioural support services, educational psychologists and advisors or teachers with a knowledge of information technology for children with special educational needs. (Code of Practice Par 2.58)

There are certain services which are mandatory, such as educational psychologists and education welfare officers; other support services are usually available from the education authority, or from franchised agencies, where funds have been delegated to schools and such services are bought back under a service level agreement. In some areas, schools have formed clusters to pool some of the devolved funding for SEN and offset the negative effects of isolation in providing for SEN. (Norwich, 1995b). Other initiatives have included setting up support groups between schools for staff development purposes.

Circular 6/94 explains in detail how these aspects must be described in the school's policy document.

> The school's policy should state the school's arrangements for securing access to external support services for pupils with special educational needs. The policy should have regard to the Code of Practice and should explain the sources from which the school seeks external specialist support and any service level agreement with the local education authority. (Circular 6/94 Par 51)

The LEA has a duty under the 1993 Act Code of Practice to inform schools of education services that are available and how these should be accessed and funded. LEAs must ascertain the demand for the SEN services from schools.

> SEN support services can play an important part in helping schools identify, access and make special educational provision for pupils with special educational needs, *not least but not only* those at Stage 3 of the five stage model described in the Code of Practice. There may be a particularly important role for such services in helping schools take early action which may prevent a pupil's learning difficulties becoming more pronounced. (Circular 6/94 Par 62)

Schools and their governors have responsibilities under the Code to identify, assess and make provision at Stages 1–3 using support services as considered necessary.

Links to other schools/integration arrangements

Schedule 1:16

> The school's SEN policy should set out any arrangements whereby the school draws upon the staff and resources of other schools, including special schools, to help the school's provision for pupils with special educational needs. Similarly, the policy should explain any arrangements which the school makes for integrating, on a part-time basis or otherwise, special school pupils in mainstream. (Circular 6/94 Par 53)

Some schools have established strong links with local special schools. This may result in a variety of arrangements to help integrate pupils from special schools into mainstream education on a part-time or temporary basis. There is an enormous variety of methods of doing this. Some involve outreach workers from the special school, others do not. Whatever arrangements are made, these should be explicit in the school's policy. If there are shared resources this too needs to be made clear. Any extra responsibilities which this gives the staff in the school concerned also needs to be clearly agreed and be written into the policy.

Links with health and social services, educational welfare and voluntary organisations

Schedule: 17

> Having regard to the Code of Practice, the school's policy should explain the school's arrangement for working with the health service, the social services department and education welfare service, together with any links the school has with local or national voluntary organisations which work on behalf of children with special educational needs. It should set out arrangements for liaison and information exchange between the SEN Co-ordinator and the designated officers of the district health authority and the social services department. (Circular 6/94 Par 56)

Child Health Services

Every LEA will be in a District Health Authority but this may well not overlap geographically with education. Health Authority personnel availability may vary, but there will be a community paediatrician and health clinics where health visitors, school nurses and speech and language therapists can be found. Local hospitals will also have a paediatric service in which physiotherapists and occupational therapists will work. Just how much hospital services can work with schools varies enormously from district to district. For troubled pupils:

> The child and adolescent mental health service is available in many areas for direct consultation. This service is available to schools for consultation and advice or for a referral for assessment. Treatment can also be undertaken. Child Guidance services where they exist, offer helpful preventative treatment and advice through advice direct to schools and teachers as well as individual pupils and their families. (Circular 9/94 Par 106)

For the SENCO, the key health worker is often the school nurse. Through her, the school doctor, therapists and other health professionals can be reached. If necessary, a special medical can be requested, whether or not the pupil is on the SEN register. At Stage 1, it is essential to consult health records; to check that hearing and vision, for example, have been examined. The school health service will have records of all school aged children and these can be accessed as necessary.

Pupils on regular medication for conditions such as asthma, diabetes or epilepsy do not have special educational needs as such, but these conditions can contribute to learning difficulties in some cases. Other pupils may have appliances which need to be maintained. An obvious example is hearing aids, which are usually checked by the LEA's hearing impaired service, who work in close co-operation with the health authority. Children with more severe disabilities will have been identified in early childhood by the health authority and the LEA will have been notified. Child community health is often the best source of information for schools.

Education Welfare Service (sometimes called Education Social Workers)

Education Welfare Officers (EWOs) are employed by the LEA to help parents and the LEA meet statutory obligations in relation to school attendance. They can play an important role with pupils who also have SEN, in helping liaise between home and school and keeping communication going in cases where attendance is sporadic. There are often underlying reasons for poor attendance which relate to learning or behavioural difficulties. Partnership between SENCOs and EWOs can be very productive in sorting out some of these underlying difficulties and easing a pupil back to school.

Social Services

Each Local Authority will have a social service department which has a children's section. It has not been very easy in the past for schools to make contact with social services on anything but a direct referral over single cases. As Campbell (1995) advises:

> Social Services departments should ensure that all schools in the area know the name of, and how to contact, a designated social services officer who has responsibility for SEN.

He further suggests that for children in care, social services officers, or foster carers' could usefully be involved in planning the IEPs for pupils at Stage 2 and above. Circular 13/94 reminds schools about pupils who are being looked after by social services departments. It suggest schools should have:

- Knowledge of the child's life/care plan.
- Close relationship and liaison with carers.
- A designated member of staff for children who are 'looked after'. Not all such children will have SEN, so may not be the responsibility of the SENCO. Liaison within school between SEN and pastoral systems will be important in these cases.

Campbell also advises that schools need to know how to contact their designated officer from social services and any referral format agreed by the social services department. The SEN policy needs to set out clearly the arrangements for working in partnership with social services and who on the school staff has responsibility for liaison, information collection and dissemination and individual planning which links to IEPs. Social services and careers services have major roles to play in transition planning for pupils with statements for SEN (see end of this chapter).

Voluntary organisations

Many disability groups have charities which concentrate on one impairment. The best known are organisations like the Royal National Institute for the Blind (RNIB), Invalid Children's Aid Nationwide (ICAN) and SCOPE (formally the Spastics Society), all of which have set up specialist schools and training of specialist teachers. There are large numbers of smaller groups specialising in a wide range of disabilities. One of the key roles of voluntary organisations is to put parents in touch with others in the same situation as themselves. This, combined with factual information about the disability, are the most important ways voluntary organisations can be used. The Council for Disabled Children in London publishes lists and contact numbers and can answer questions about a whole range of children's problems. Some addresses are given in **Source List 3, p.123**. There are also local generic groups supporting parents and children with all types of SEN. Local addresses should be available from Schools Psychological Services (SPS) or the education officer for SEN. Parent partnership officers, being appointed in many LEAs, will also have contacts. SENCOs need to build up a database of local and national organisations which include named contacts, with telephone numbers.

Many of these voluntary groups are now acting as befrienders to parents going through Stages 4 and 5 of the assessment process and may in the future become 'named persons'. As Marsh (1995) states, schools and LEAs will have to be satisfied that these volunteers have the essential attributes to become 'named persons', which, in his view, are:

- Good listening and communication skills.
- Reliability, availability, 'stickability'.
- Knowledge of child and family.
- Understanding of the legal framework.
- Independence, in terms of having no connection with the LEA, and also being confident enough to disagree with the parent.

The 'named person' is defined in the glossary of the Code of Practice, but this role has yet to worked out in full. The concept is to provide parents with someone who can give advice and information. The training of 'named persons' is being developed in many LEAs sometimes by the parent partnership officer.

There is a difference between using a 'named person' to help the parent and give advice and being an advocate on behalf of a parent or a group. Some voluntary organisations provide an advocacy role, the Independent Panel for Special Educational Advice (IPSEA), for example. Marsh (1995) describes these organisations as 'seeking to empower parents so that they can gain confidence in becoming partners with professionals in supporting their child.' The theme of working with parents will be continued in Chapter 9.

The SENCOs role in developing multi-disciplinary partnerships

Keeping a file

Each SENCO needs to know what is available locally from education, health and social services and the voluntary sector. There should be a file in school giving basic information with names and contact numbers for all the agencies and services and how referrals can be made. It may be useful to include the addresses and contacts of special schools, as they too have expertise and may be able to offer advice. See the list of support services and agencies at the end of this chapter.

Support services and agencies linked to SEN work

Education	Health	Social Services
Educational Psychologists	Community Services	Children's Services (sometimes part of generic service)
Educational Welfare Officers	School Nurse/Doctor	Child Care Officer
Education Officer (statements) or equivalent	Health Visitors (pre-school)	Disability Services or part of generic
Behaviour Support Services	Speech and Language Therapists	Day Nurseries
Learning Support Services	Community Paediatrician	
Teachers for the: Hearing Impaired Visually Impaired less frequently: Language Impaired Physically Impaired	*Hospital Services* Hospital Paediatrician Occupational Therapist Physiotherapist	
Advisory Teachers for SEN	Child and Family Clinics (Psychiatry)	
Portage Service for pre-school children		Specialist doctors and Assessment centres
Pupil Referral Units		
Home Tuition Service		
Hospital Teachers		
Parent Partnership Officer		
Named person group (voluntary) but set up by LEA or above officer.		
Careers Service (some privatised)		

Purposes of contributions from outside services and agencies

Once information about what is available locally and how it can be accessed is known, the next step for SENCOs is to define the purposes for which these outside agencies and services might be useful. Diamond suggests LEA support services will be most use if they:

- Support SENCOs in their work as 'a critical friend'.
- Remain practical at a classroom level, enskilling teachers with strategies to support SEN.
- Help embed delivery of support by working within the National Curriculum, seeing the IEP as an extension of normal classroom planning cycles.
- Provide school-focused and school-based in-service training to staff, remaining flexible to the needs of SENCOs and staff.

At Stage 3 and above

- Provide individual assessment and observation usually at Stage 3 after attending at Stage 2 reviews. This will be most useful if it helps schools to define targets and give ideas for strategies to meet these targets.
- Provide direct teaching or practical support to pupils and teachers.
- Give ideas for intervention strategies to manage behaviour, training staff in relation to emotional and behavioural difficulties.

Both Health and Education will:

- Carry out formal assessments for Stage 4 after a request from the LEA for Appendix reports towards the statementing process. (See Appendix 8a)
- Support parents and families, particularly at Stages 3-5. Support to parents may include helping those with attendance problems.
- Give advice and support to pupils with a range of disabilities particularly at Stages 3 and 5.
- Provide direct therapies (speech and language, occupational or physiotherapy) or specialist support or teaching including provision and use of specialist equipment, IT etc. For this to be effective advice needs to contribute to classroom practice and access to the National Curriculum.
- Contribute to case conferences and annual reviews of pupils.

It is probably at Stage 3 that the SENCO's role in working collaboratively with colleagues and support services becomes most important. SENCOs need to be proactive in planning IEP for Stage 3 pupils and getting to know who will be the best outside agent to help in the process. As Diamond (1995) states,

> It is essential that the providers of SEN services to schools can articulate for themselves what characterises their distinctive contribution to the identification, assessment and making of provision in schools. Services can be agents of change but only if they work with a preventative role. (p.65)

At Stage 5 the LEA must 'supply or arrange for SEN support services in support of a pupil who has a statement of SEN and whose need for the support service is specified in the statement, if funds for the support service have not been delegated to the school'. All maintained schools (i.e. GM and LEA) must have equal access to such services.

Referrals to outside services

From the above it is clear that, as part of their SEN policy, schools need to develop their procedures for referrals and requests to support services and agencies. Where there are a number of possible choices, decisions need to be made about the best route for support and advice. Over referral to a number of agencies at one time, for the same case, is ineffective and wasteful of scarce resources.

Each service will have a specialism and if possible this should guide the school's choice. Some learning support services will have a range of specialists in their teams. Referrals to the service may initially be through the regular key worker, but that person will know someone else who can help in special cases. For example, educational psychologists usually have good contacts with health and social services and may be the first contact for many referrals. On the other hand, some specialist services e.g. hearing and vision prefer direct contact. It is up to each service to make the referral routes clear to schools and parents.

It is also important in school to keep a record of who has been asked to help for any one child. This should be part of the paperwork attached to the IEP. Good practice is to have a top sheet in each file listing outside agency involvement and dates and indicate if a report is attached. Such a top sheet should be used from Stage 1 or 2 of the staged assessment process, so a cumulative record is kept (see Appendix 8b). Communication within the school about referrals is vital, especially when traditionally some services are used by the pastoral systems and others by the learning support department. There have been cases where, for example, a pupil has been excluded and the SENCO was not asked to contribute what was known about the pupil's difficulties and who was already involved. In all individual cases, if outside services or agencies are given referrals by a school, the parents or guardian must be informed and in the majority of cases give permission. Services can support staff rather than the pupils, in which case of course, parental permission would be inappropriate.

Getting to know key workers from health/social services

Because of the focus of their work, health or social service personnel may have different priorities from those of the school. This will effect their management of time and who they perceive as the client. It may be difficult to get support for teachers and the school, when it is the child or family that, in the service's view should receive their expertise. One way to overcome potential professional barriers is to get to know the individual worker on an informal basis outside of the case conference or meeting situation. Inviting professionals to school staff meetings to explain their roles and share ideas with teachers can be very helpful. Joint working practices can then be decided and then, when there is a problem to be solved, this joint understanding will give better results. The school nurse, for example, is a resource that is undervalued in many schools, but therapists and other health and social work professionals may also be persuaded to visit schools on a one-off basis as part of an awareness training session. McKinlay (1995) reminds SENCOs that school health staff should be encouraged to communicate with teachers in the interest of the children.

Parents as part of multi-professional network

Parents need to know about outside services and agencies and have these various roles explained, especially if there is multi-agency involvement. Again this is best done informally but should be invoked before the parent has to face a room full of strangers at an annual review or a case conference. Parents themselves may be the SENCO's best source of information. If the child has been known to the health service since pre-school years, then the parent will know key workers from the community health or the hospitals who have already worked with the child and provided advice.

For very complex disability cases the parent often is the **key worker** for their child, linking the therapies and advice together into an individual plan. Be sure this expertise is valued by yourself and the school and taken into account when asking for yet more to be done at home. In very complex cases the child may be known to up to thirty or so professionals. There will be notes kept by each one in their own files but it is the parent who has the total picture. In cases where, for example, three therapists require programmes of practice at home, there may not be time for the 'just ten minutes' practice from school as well.

Ensuring effective support

For schools, the best professional advice is that which helps to contribute to the child's IEP in a practical way. For pupils with statements, the advice will have informed the statement writer who will have then listed the needs and priority objectives for the school to achieve. On receipt of such a full statement, targets must be set by the school which will be reviewed at the annual review. The same model should apply to Stage 3 advice after assessment. The information given should help the school choose a range of appropriate targets to be achieved and a means by which these can be assessed when reached.

If the report from the professional is full of jargon and results of tests unknown to the school, this is not helpful. It will be necessary to enquire of the report writer:

- What will this do to help us in the classroom?
- What is reasonable to expect of this pupil?
- How will we know if the result is sufficient and whether the targets have been reached (i.e. success criteria)?

Support by giving advice on strategies

The overwhelming demand from teachers, when getting outside advice and support, is for strategies to meet the targets set, and this within the structure of a normal school day and the National Curriculum. Some services therefore, though excellent for assessment, do not directly support teachers or SENCOs. They may help tease out any within-child factors e.g. medical reasons for a problem. These services are either from the medical professions or are working on a 'medical model' even from within education.

An understanding of the curriculum and the social context of the classroom and school is also needed, if staff are to be fully supported in meeting the needs of more complex individuals. Often what is needed is ideas for or actual examples of extra resources or technology to use with the pupil. Staff may need to borrow equipment for a short time to try it out and many will need training about how it should be used. If equipment only is given and no training, it may just sit in a cupboard for most or all of the time. IT in particular can help so many pupils with SEN, but knowing which equipment to buy and whether it will fit the pupils' needs is an expert job. Over time schools develop this expertise themselves but they need someone to call on with complex problems. The SENCO may have to keep tracks on the extra resources provided or borrowed and be accountable for their efficient use.

The school/service working partnership

Contracts and service agreements

Certain support services may visit on a very regular basis, others only on one-off visits. Where the service is regular it is good practice to set up a contract or service level agreement with each service. This should state the priority for the work over the next term and list the names and stages on the SEN register of pupils who will receive support, and if necessary note other agencies working in relation to the named pupils. Clear definitions of purpose should be made and very clear descriptions agreed about what the service will provide and how the school will support this delivery. Time available from the service to the school should be clearly stated, so both sides fulfil the promises. For example, the school must inform the service in good time of closures or special events such as field trips which would make the delivery to a particular child impossible. The service must give information on changes of day or time and of illness of the worker. Each agreement needs to set a review date where the SENCO and the support service teacher can sit down and evaluate the quality of the service given. This review should be at least half yearly.

On call services

Other services expect to be 'on call', but will appreciate as much notice as possible. Some situations are emergencies but most are not, so 'on call' services need to be given an idea of how urgent the request is and a reasonable time-scale agreed. Planning is needed, for example, to prepare reports for annual reviews in good time to be circulated before the meeting. At least two months notice is therefore needed if the teacher or service member must visit the child before writing the report.

Clusters with other schools

Where SEN funding has been devolved under LMS schemes in some cases this has resulted in schools not being in a position to buy back a useful level of support services. The result across a district can then be the potential loss of available services. One response to this problem has been to form clusters to pool resources and inset ideas on decision making for SEN. Clusters are defined by Norwich (1995b) as:

> a grouping of schools with a relatively stable and long term commitment to share some resources and decision making about an area of activity. The arrangements are likely to involve a degree of formality such as regular meetings to plan and monitor this activity and some loss of autonomy through the need for negotiated decision making. (p.25)

Examples of working clusters are described in more detail in *Working together* (Lunt et al, 1994).

There are a number of puzzling pupils for whom it isn't quite clear what is needed. Often the best and most effective way to support will be to work with teachers rather than pupils to enhance the teachers' own professional skills in managing all the pupils and their classes. The Audit Commission, 1992 states:

> Success of support teams should not always be measured only by pupil progress. Schools may require both direct and indirect support and general guidance. Evaluation should take account of any role in increasing schools' capacities for managing pupils with SEN. Par 86, p.55

Therefore, services will be at their most effective if they can be seen to increase the school's capacity for meeting SEN. This means services must meet teachers' as well as child needs. If a teacher feels supported by knowledge that she/he is doing the right thing and can see the pupil taking a full part in school life and making progress, this will have been a piece of effective support. If, on the other hand, the expert advice has puzzled, confused or deskilled the teacher, the support will be worse than useless, it could be harmful. The overarching purpose for support should be to support the teacher to support the child. The above applies to working with parents. School support services cannot focus on the parents' adult needs, but they can support parents to support their children.

Working in partnership at transition periods

The SENCO needs to take a strong lead in helping colleagues to plan both entry and departure from the school for pupils with SEN. These are key points in the pupil's life and good planning, record keeping and communication can make a great deal of difference to their wellbeing. There are three critical action times;

- *Entry to school* – planned entry is necessary for children identified pre-school as having special educational needs with or without a statement.
- *Transition between phases* – usually primary/secondary although infant/junior or first/middle should be added in some LEAs.
- *Leaving school* – for college or adult life. This involves the transition plan for pupils with statements but should be planned for all pupils with identified SEN.

All of these can involve working in a multi-disciplinary partnership and need describing as part of the school's policy.

Early years

Certain children have their special needs identified shortly after birth or before they are two or three years old. Health professionals will have taken the lead in this identification process and will have informed the LEA, who then can carry out multi-professional assessments for a statement and will do so for those whose needs warrant this and when the parent agrees. Education offers some services pre-school, usually a Portage home visiting service which works directly with parents using a developmental checklist to identify the next learning step. Services of hearing and vision also visit as soon as the disability is diagnosed. There may be places for children with special needs in opportunity playgroups or nursery classes, but sometimes the only education available will have been a special school's nursery. Planning entry to school from this variety of provision requires good liaison from all concerned. Usually some joint planning has taken place with the SENCO or class teacher, using the knowledge gained by the personnel who will have worked with the child and family before school entry. Many LEAs have an under-fives multi-disciplinary panel which can give advice about a child's needs to the receiving school.

There are important issues about entry to school for these more vulnerable children. Arrangements need to be flexible and offer a gradual entry into the full-time experience of school life. For example, the child may come for only part of the day or perhaps not go into the playground with all the older children. This may ease the shock of being with large numbers of bigger children. Ancillary helpers are of great importance in easing in these young children. Parents have a vital role to play in this planned entry. Robson (1989) offers further practical help to those planning entry to school, pp.142-145. The Code of Practice section 5, gives further information about pre-school special needs and preparation for school in Par 5.29.

This means that those children without statements may need to be put on the school's SEN register at Stage 2 or 3 on entry. This does not necessarily mean proceeding onto Stage 4, but it will mean that an IEP is in place from entry to school. Such planning should help to build on what has already been done and help make a smooth transition to school. It is therefore essential that good use is made of pre-school records in planning to build on existing achievements. There must be no reluctance on the part of teachers to read and use any information available from all sources including parents.

Transition between phases

Primary/Secondary Phases

For pupils with a range of SEN, planned transfer between schools is essential. The school organising the department needs to make personal contact with the new school wherever possible, but should always make sure all records, including SEN records, are up-to-date and sent on in good time. A planning meeting, either at an annual review for a pupil with a statement, or an IEP review for others, should include parents and if possible someone from the new school. Support services have a vital role in easing transition and helping the new school make plans. Often, the same support teacher may be able to support the pupil in the new school, but even when this is not possible another member of the team may do so. The receiving school must read all records in good time so that plans are in place before entry, especially for the more vulnerable pupils. This is usually well done for those with sensory or physical disabilities. Support services and health personnel typically plan what equipment is needed and discuss mobility issues. Planning for pupils with learning or emotional difficulties is often much weaker. Yet for these pupils, poor preparation may result in a setback to learning, or in extreme cases such a traumatic start at the new school that the pupil never settles.

Transition plans at 14+

Good planning will also be needed for many pupils at Stages 2/3, to ease transfer into Further Education Colleges and again support services can be asked to help. But for pupils with statements, at the first annual review after the young person's 14th birthday, a transition plan *must* be included.

Transition plans start in Year 9 and continue annually until the young person leaves school. It is important that all professionals involved build good relationships with the young person and their families and give them all information about what is available in their local area. The LEA must involve social services and the careers service and consult child health and any other relevant professionals, such as educational psychologists and therapists.

Russell (1995) states that the challenge of the transition plan lies in development of continuity of assessment, review and programme planning from school through further educational, vocational and personal preparation for a valued and productive adult life. Thus:

- Co-ordinating the many different agencies and professions which can contribute to this process.
- Creating positive approaches to participation by students and parents in assessment and planning for transition.
- Transferring information and expertise between phases and agencies involved in transition.
- Providing advocacy and advice directly to young people at a time of major changes in their family life and educational experience. (p.58)

The Code of Practice, par 6:59 makes it very clear that the young person should be actively involved in the development of the transition plan. As Gascoigne (1995) points out this may be the first time that the young person is consulted without parents being present. She suggests that parents may find this period very stressful as their feelings are ambivalent. 'On the one hand they want their child to become as independent as possible, and on the other, they wish to extend their protection of them' (p. 138). Both Gascoigne and Russell emphasise how sensitive parents can be and how much support they will need from those working with them.

Social Services must (under Schedule 1 of the Children Act 1989) give information on:

- Full range of services for children and young people within the area for those deemed as being 'in need'.
- Local opportunities for leisure and other activities.
- Practical advice on benefits, aids and adaptations to the home.
- Counselling and advocacy services.
- Arrangements for multi-disciplinary assessment and care plans for those seen as having significant needs.
- Transport arrangements and specific skills training, for example, mobility.

They must also inform young people being looked after of their rights to Post-18 support. (Par 6:48–6:52 Code of Practice).

Careers Services must give information on:

- Realistic careers choices and training opportunities and employment.
- Available support from a range of professionals.
- Strategies for supporting independence and social skills training needs.

Specialist careers officers will provide advice on all the options, including residential provision for young people with special needs. Information must be updated regularly. Careers information will be given in a form that is accessible to young people with special needs, e.g. Large print, tapes or computer software with pictures and sound. (Par 6:53–6:54 Code of Practice)

LEA/Schools must give information on:

- Local Post-16 College courses and training opportunities.
- FEFC assessment and funding arrangements (in Circular 95/07 Students with Learning Difficulties or Disabilities), FEFC, Cheylesmore House, Quinton Road, Coventry, CV1 2WT.

- Advice about the range of professionals who can ensure expert advice.
- Make sure the young person with SEN has an interview with a careers officer. This should be considered for some pupils at Stage 3 as well as those with a statement, if necessary from the specialist careers officer.
- The careers officer attends or provides written input for all 14+ reviews.
- All those with parental responsibility should have access to the Specialist careers officer and contribute to the plan.
- Make sure the young person's views are taken into account on all decisions.
- Make use of positive forms of recording, such as Records of Achievement, which represent the young person's strengths and information about wider interests and abilities.
- Involve all other relevant professionals and annual reviews post-14, including members of social services. (Par 6:55–6:58 Code of Practice)
- Schools also need to build links to local further education colleges. Sometimes link provision can be arranged to give opportunities for integration into the adult environment of further education.

Concluding thoughts

This chapter has described in some detail the complexity of working within a multi-professional network. SENCOs will need to develop their own style of working which fits the context of their school and LEA. What is available will vary enormously from district to district. It will take time to learn what is on offer and to get to know the people concerned. Internal school organisation also varies enormously. In some schools, heads and senior managers deal with the outside agencies, in others it is the SENCO. Whatever the system, *communication will be the key issue if the SENCO is to carry out their role effectively.*

CHAPTER 8

Paperwork and Procedures: the Co-ordinating Role

This chapter links up with Chapter 3 on identification and intervention and looks at the co-ordinating role of the SENCO in relation to all the paperwork and procedures required by the whole of the Code of Practice, but particularly at Stages 3 to 5. The SENCO must take responsibility for managing their school's record keeping systems for all those with SEN, take a lead role in organising the reviews of IEPs for stages 2 and 3, and the annual reviews for those with the statements. The SENCO is also likely to have responsibility for monitoring outcomes of these reviews. The Code of Practice has made great demands on SENCOs in terms of resources of time and their management abilities. This chapter describes ideas gathered from practice about ways of organising paperwork, holding reviews and setting targets for pupils with SEN in partnership with pupils, parents and colleagues. The chapter ends with descriptions of two special situations in which SENCOs might be asked to help prepare paperwork, a) for SEN tribunals, b) for OFSTED inspections.

All of the above should be reflected in how roles and responsibilities are allocated and evaluated as part of the school's SEN policy. This was described in Chapter 2 and will be revisited in the last chapter. One of the issues for large schools, particularly in the secondary phase, is how much of this responsibility can reasonably or efficiently be given to the SENCO and how the SENCO will communicate with others, particularly those in the pastoral team, the head and governors.

The work described here is perceived as an important part of the co-ordinating role, though not necessarily to be carried out by the SENCO alone. The head has the ultimate responsibility to see that these tasks are carried out effectively, and in turn must report to the governors on their effectiveness. The tasks required include:

- The management of the files for all pupils on the SEN register.
- The management of IEP reviews for those on Stages 2 or 3, usually on a termly basis but at least twice a year.
- Organising paperwork for a request for multi-disciplinary assessments at Stage 4.

- Contributing to Appendix D when requested by the LEA for a Stage 5 assessment.
- Setting of targets within two months of receipt of the statement – designing an IEP for each pupil with a statement in conjunction with relevant staff.
- Monitoring and reviewing all IEPs on Stages 2–5.
- Holding annual reviews for pupils with statements. This is the responsibility of the head teacher but in practice is often delegated to the SENCO. In any case both head and SENCO need to know the procedures.
- Working with the LEA on transition plans at 14+ annual reviews.
- Supporting the head if she/he is requested to attend a tribunal, by helping prepare paperwork.
- Supporting the head in preparing paperwork for an OFSTED inspection.

All of the above will require organisation skills and clarity of purpose. It will also call on interpersonal skills of dealing with a range of people: the child, parent, teacher and other professionals. This consultative work will be covered in more depth in the next chapter. The present chapter will concentrate on the 'bureaucratic' aspect of the work.

Organisation of files

It may sound mundane or even trivial but a lot rests on how and where files are stored, how accessible these are to SENCO and staff alike. There is no single correct way to do this, each school needs to work out the system which works for them and then to make it clear within their policy document. Examples of ways it could be done are:

- Have one filing system in the school office with a subsection in each file labelled SEN register file or colour coded. This will work if the filing system is accessible both to relevant staff and visiting professionals but is secure. It will not work if the room is locked when office staff leave in the evening and the teachers and SENCO cannot gain access.
Or:
- Have a separate SEN register fling cabinet in the SENCO's room which is accessible to teachers and visiting professionals as relevant. This means the main file also needs marking to indicate there is a SEN file elsewhere. Duplication of the file is likely to be expensive. It makes a segregated record system which may be difficult to cross-reference.
Or:
- Put the SEN register on a computer file along with factual details, but see the current IEP as a working document, kept by teachers. File IEPs after review in main files as a SEN subsection.
Or:
- Devolve all SEN filing to class teachers/year departments, and ask them to write IEPs and review them.

It still would be wise to keep a management form to collate information about the number of schools a child has attended, guardian names, number of outside professionals involved and dates of reviews (see Appendix 8b example). This system still needs checking by the SENCO who is responsible for seeing reviews are held and paperwork kept in order. The SENCO cannot distance themselves too much from the review process particularly at Stage 3 where they have a key role to play.

The register

The SEN register must contain, as a minimum, the list of names of pupils at each of the Code of Practice stages. Many schools keep other information on the SEN register as well, such as short notes about the type of SEN each pupil may have, whether English is their first language and date of the last IEP review. The LEA can request a copy of the register and some LEAs use this data to help allocate SEN formula funding under LMS schemes, usually after some form of moderation. OFSTED inspectors will also request to see SEN registers along with other paperwork for SEN.

Organisation of IEP reviews

Of all aspects of the Code of Practice, this is the most challenging to schools. Running these reviews is very time consuming for the class or subject teacher as well as the SENCO. If parents' views are to be fully incorporated, this too represents an enormous commitment of time for schools. The number of pupils who require IEP reviews has risen in larger schools to over one hundred. It is possible that too many pupils are being identified at these levels of the Code. Many LEAs have developed triggers, or threshold descriptions for each level and within each type of difficulty or disability. These triggers suggest that a rigorous assessment of need should take place before letting pupils move forward a stage and an equally rigorous review held to see if they can return to a lower stage, as a result of progress made.

The whole strength of the staged assessment procedure depends on this review process being regular, thorough, and recorded on paper. Teachers are complaining about the level of bureaucracy involved and saying it doesn't benefit themselves or their pupils. It is up to schools to develop ways which work for teachers and pupils, while still complying with the main principles of the Code of Practice. These are to identify and meet needs of all pupils with any special need and to give them full access to the curriculum and life of the school. Good assessment makes for good teaching, so the IEP process must work to improve teaching and learning outcomes.

The IEP as a process of continuous assessment

There is a great debate in schools about what constitutes an IEP. It clearly must be envisaged as a process and a set of documents. Writing one beautiful plan will not suffice; it is the setting and evaluating of the targets over time that makes an IEP valuable to the pupil. The key questions are:

- What does *this* pupil need as a priority to help them make progress in the curriculum? What are the pupil's and the parents' views?
- What level has the pupil already reached? (State existing levels of attainment, reading age, National Curriculum levels, in as precise a way as possible).
- What can the child do? What strengths have they? Use National Curriculum level descriptions wherever possible.
- What are the logical next steps to be achieved within the priority areas chosen? i.e. set targets. These need to be decided with the pupil wherever possible.
- How will these targets be achieved? Describe strategies and resources required, including frequency and timing of support.
- How will the targets be evaluated to see if they have been achieved? State method of evaluation or assessment. This last will help the review process. If the targets are not set in precise enough terms, it will be impossible to know if they were or were not achieved.

- Decide who will monitor all of the above and how progress will be recorded.

At the review, check which targets are reached, which are partially reached and which have not been possible. Then set new targets. These could be the same ones again with different success criteria or they could be new targets, depending on what was perceived as success and what had been difficult. The conditions under which success was achieved need to be stated. If the pupil only made progress when given support in class or through a specific programme of intervention, these methods need to be noted. This is particularly important at Stages 3–5.

IEP reviews also need to be held regularly, probably twice a term, for pupils with statements. Some may be 'mini reviews' with the support teacher and class teacher only, others may require SENCO or parents present. The targets for pupils with statements will have been set first within two months of receipt of the statement or as part of the annual review process. The Code of Practice does not spell this out, but tribunal case law is suggesting that IEPs are required for all statemented pupils. It certainly makes sense to give the pupils with the most needs at least the same degree of planning as is required at earlier stages. (**See a staff development exercise in Activity 5.**)

Holding a Stage 3 review to consider moving to Stage 4

Many pupils can remain on Stage 3 for some time, but Stage 3 is characterised by the involvement of outside support services and agencies, so it is unlikely that there will be resources available for many pupils to be at this stage for more than a year or so. Either the pupil will be making some progress and can return to Stage 2, or will not be making significant progress and the decision may then be made to ask the LEA to consider a multi-disciplinary assessment at Stage 4.

At the Stage 3 review where Stage 4 is being considered, parents' views must be sought and the process of requesting a multi-disciplinary assessment explained in detail. The purpose of the assessment needs to be explained and the possibility that the LEA a) may not agree to the assessment, or b) may not issue a statement, explained along with their right to appeal.

The support professional or agencies who have been involved at Stage 3 should contribute to this Stage 3 review. They will be asked for evidence as part of the Stage 4 assessment and their views are needed in this Stage 3 review. It is possible that the LEA's trigger for a Stage 4 will be known to the support personnel who can advise schools as to whether this case meets these triggers. Parents can make requests independently of schools or any support services, but schools will be required to give evidence about which services or agencies have been involved. Only a very small proportion of children will require a statement, (approx. 1 per cent) so their needs must be significant to warrant this final assessment.

Most LEAs have set quite stringent criteria for Stage 4 assessments which they will have published. LEAs often have proformas they wish schools to complete when requesting a formal Stage 4 assessment. The Code of Practice states very clearly that it is the head teacher's responsibility to make the decision to request a final assessment, unless a parent has already done so. This is, however usually done in close co-operation with the SENCO. The LEA will need evidence of the pupil's needs and about what the school has already done to meet that need. Copies of IEPs and reviews must be sent along with a summary paragraph stating why a Stage

4 assessment is requested.

Schools will be asked to write what is known as Appendix D as their contribution to the Stage 4 assessment. All the advice will be attached to the draft statement, issued at Stage S and will be part of the document known as the statement (see Appendix 8a). Most LEAs will have a proforma which schools are asked to use when supplying an Appendix D. It will usually cover the following sections and ask for information as below.

Contributions to school's advice for Stage 4 assessment (Appendix D)

Part A

Background Information Give information about how long the child has been in your school and when the difficulties were first noted. Summarise with dates, the child's movement through Stages 1–3, identify outside agencies involvement and any support/provision given by the school to date.

Current Functioning: Identify skills in each area giving National Curriculum levels where appropriate. Describe areas of strength as well as difficulties. Use headings: reading, numeracy, language and subject headings if appropriate. Include descriptions of learning style and response to teaching. Describe behaviour and social skills and the child's relationship to adults and peers.

Other Factors: In this section mention any other factors such as attendance or medical history that might be relevant. Summarise relationship with family and parents' perceptions of the child's needs. Parents will be asked by the LEA to give their views in full in other appendices.

Part B: Special Educational Needs

Summarise on the basis of the above information, your perception of the pupil's strengths and special educational needs. Be as specific as possible.

Part C: Aims of Provision

Identify what you perceive would be the long term aim of any provision given to the child by a statement. Link these aims to the needs identified in Part B.

Part D: Resources

Comment on facilities and resources which you believe the child will need to fulfil the aims identified in Part C. Finally, include equipment (e.g. IT), ideas about differentiation/modification or support. Who would monitor these arrangements?

While an assessment is taking place the pupil continues to have IEPs written and reviewed as on Stage 3. The LEA is required to complete their assessment in six months under the Code. Their decision can be to make a statement with or without resources, or to issue a 'note in lieu'. In the later case the pupil returns to Stage 3, but with the information from the note to inform teachers of the pupil's needs.

Setting targets on receipt of a final statement

When the school receives the final statement, they have two months in which to set targets for the first year and to send a copy of these to the LEA. In practice, schools need to develop IEPs for pupils with statements. These will be largely concerned with putting the targets into practice. Pupil views will need to be recorded and a careful record kept of how targets are evaluated. These targets will need to be reviewed regularly, probably twice termly, and all those who teach the pupil kept informed of the revised targets. In large schools, this will require a system to both collect, collate and share information to and from the learning support team (see **Activity** 5). This system could also be useful for pupils at Stages 2 and 3. This will all contribute to the annual review where parents and professional viewpoints will also be collected and where new targets will be set.

Annual Reviews

The full details of annual review procedures are published in Part 6 of the Code of Practice. Every child who has a statement of SEN must have this statement reviewed by the LEA at least annually. To do this, the LEA requires the head teacher to submit a review report by a specified date. The LEA must give at least two months notice of the date by which the report is required.

> Before producing the report the head teacher must convene a meeting to assist in its preparation. The head teacher must write to parents and relevant staff members, any people identified by the LEA and anyone else the head teacher considers appropriate; and must circulate copies of the advice received before the meeting. Following the meeting the head teacher must submit the review report to the LEA by the specified date. Regulation 15(5) and 10.

The head may delegate responsibility for running the review meeting, but must be sure the teacher knows of all those from health and social services who should be invited.

What must be done in advance of the review date?

At least two months in advance of the meeting the head must request written advice from:

- the child's parents;
- those the LEA has specified;
- those the head teacher considers appropriate.

These are likely to be, the class and support teacher or assistant, any specialist teacher giving advice or an educational psychologist, any health and social service professionals involved with the child.

The head must then circulate all the written advice to those who are attending the meeting, inviting additional comments including comments from those invited to attend. The time scale for these reports is important. Visiting professionals are unlikely to want to write a report without visiting the school to see the child. They will need to fit this into a busy schedule and must be given maximum notice of the dates by which their advice is needed. Parents may need support on submitting their advice and may welcome a pre-review meeting especially if it is the first annual review after the statement was made or at transition times when their child is due to change school.

An informal meeting may prepare the parent for the much bigger and more formal review meeting. Parents usually find annual reviews stressful, so the preparation meeting can answer questions and ensure that parents feel confident that their views have been noted. On the day of the meeting, the room should be prepared with sufficient chairs arranged so parents, their friend and child, if present, can sit together and near a known teacher or other member of staff. The room should be one where there will not be interruptions to interfere with the meeting.

At the Review Meeting

The head or chairperson introduces themselves and others and makes clear the purpose of the annual review meeting, which is to:

- Make sure the parents' views are heard.
- Make sure the child's views are heard.
- Consider the teachers' reports of progress towards statement targets or those set by previous annual review.
- Consider advice from other professionals including those not present.
- Note any changes in the child's circumstances.
- Consider current provision.
- Decide on suitable targets for the coming year.
- Consider any further actions required and by whom.
- Decide if the statement is appropriate or needs amendment by the LEA.
- Decide if the statement should continue or cease to be maintained.

After the Review

The head must prepare the review report which summarises the outcomes of the review meeting and sets targets for the coming year. The head must circulate this report to all those concerned with the review. The LEA must then review the statement in the light of the report and may recommend amendments to a statement if:

> 1. Significant new needs have emerged which are not recorded on the statement.
> 2. Significant needs which are recorded on the statement are no longer present.
> 3. The provision should be amended to meet the child's changing needs and the targets specified at the review meeting, or
> 4. The child should change schools, either at the point of transfer between school phases, for example infant to junior or primary to secondary, or when a child's needs would more appropriately be met in a different school, for example by integration in the mainstream. Code of Practice, Par 6:28

Schools' role in tribunal cases

When parents wish to appeal against the LEA's decisions regarding making an assessment or the provision given in the final statement or for the other reasons listed in *How to Make an Appeal* (DfE 1994e), they can do so to the SEN tribunal (see Chapter 9 for fuller explanation). The tribunal is chaired by a lawyer and has two lay members drawn from education or associated professions. The tribunal has extensive powers. It can require witnesses to attend, or ask for access to records of the child's work at request of the parties. In most cases it is the head teacher who attends at the LEA's request. They may be asked questions such as, how the school allocates their resources from the SEN budget, how support is organised and how the curriculum is differentiated to match the IEP targets. Parents may ask any member of the school's staff to attend as their witness and they must do so if subpoenaed.

It is wise therefore, to have an agreed policy, not only for ordinary complaints to the school, but for cases where the parent may appeal against an LEA decision. The head teacher, who holds the overall responsibility for the SEN policy, may need to produce evidence or attend the tribunal. The SENCO may be expected to help to produce this evidence in the form of well kept records, showing both the pupil's progress and the types of intervention and support given by the school. Pupil and parents' views over time will be an important part of this evidence. Class teachers will sometimes be required to produce evidence of curriculum work of the pupil. Sometimes schools may agree with the parents' appeal to the tribunal against the LEA, in other situations schools might agree with the LEA. The school can feel caught between the LEA and the parent, and so the whole context of the tribunal hearing and its preparation can cause stress for all concerned.

For these reasons, it is important that two things always happen where parents may feel they need to appeal against an LEA's decision, by requesting a tribunal hearing. Firstly, the paperwork should be in good order, showing IEPs in place and reviewed over time. This applies to pupils with a statement even more than those at earlier stages. Secondly, everything should be done to maintain normal professional relationships with the parent, their befriender or named person. This does not mean that staff should agree with everything about the parent's appeal, indeed the school should make its position clear to the parent. The decision at the tribunal will be binding and the LEA must comply with instructions given by the tribunal. Therefore in many cases, relationships between school and parents are likely to have to continue after the hearing is over.

Preparing for an OFSTED inspection

The inspection team will be looking at how the school's policy and provision is working. They will determine how far:

- Provision for SEN permeates the school's organisational and curriculum structures and practice.
- All staff work closely with the SENCO.
- Parents know who is the SENCO and who is the responsible person (head or special governor).
- Resources, including staffing are managed effectively and efficiently to support SEN policies and pupils' identified needs.
- All staff are sufficiently aware of procedures for identifying, assessing and providing for pupils with SEN.
- In-service has been given to staff about SEN in the previous two years.
- Pupils' progress is monitored, especially in relation to annual reviews and IEPs.
- Assessment, recording and reporting satisfy statutory requirements.
- The use of specialist support from outside agencies is well managed within the school. The OFSTED Framework (1995).

Before the inspection

Before the inspection, the head sends paperwork to the registered inspector. This will include factual, numerical and financial information about the school and must include information about National Curriculum assessment. The registered inspector will also meet with parents without members of staff or the head being present.

During the inspection

- Inspectors may examine a sample of statements, annual reviews and IEPs from those on the SEN register.
- They will be looking to see whether the curriculum planning and implementation take account of pupils' SEN. Particular attention will be paid to whether the curriculum for pupils with SEN meets the specific needs identified in the learning objectives in IEPs.
- They should note whether specialised resources or adaptation to accommodation, furniture and acoustics have been made, including the use of technological communication aids, when these are specified for individuals.
- They will determine whether pupils with SEN have equality of access to the National Curriculum and opportunities to make progress. Pupils' access to the curriculum should not be compromised by withdrawal for additional support of learning difficulties.

The inspection team will evaluate the extent to which the school is staffed and resourced to teach the curriculum effectively. Staffing for SEN pupils with statements should reflect levels in guidance given in Circular 11/90.

Preparation by the SENCO for an OFSTED inspection

The SENCO is likely to be given some time to meet inspectors and should have the following documents and information to hand.

- The SEN register showing information about numbers of pupils at each of the
- stages.
- The SEN policy giving information about the school as listed in Schedule 1 (see Appendix 2b).
- School prospectus and other communications with parents, such as standard letters.
- Support timetables showing how support is deployed, monitored and evaluated.
- Staffing information; job descriptions for support staff. (The SENCO is only a part of the learning support system and others may be responsible for support management.)
- Systems of passing information to and from staff should be clearly explained. This should include ways IEPs are reviewed and how parents' and pupils' views are incorporated.
- Information about in-service about SEN in the last two years.
- Minutes of relevant meetings.
- Links with other schools or colleges. Information about the use of outside agencies and services.
- Information about the SEN budget. Inspectors will be looking at the 'value for money' aspect of the SEN provision. SENCOs should know their own department's budget and be able to discuss the school's priorities for resourcing SEN.

The head and governors however, continue to hold overall responsibility for determining the policy and approach to SEN and for setting up appropriate funding and staffing arrangements. The governors' annual report must inform parents about the success of the SEN policy and any significant changes and the allocation of resources over the previous year to pupils with SEN. It is not the SENCO's role to determine budgets or policies, but it will be useful if their advice is sought by governors and if in turn, the SENCO understands the main principles which the governors apply in deciding how resources will be allocated between and amongst pupils with SEN.

Summary

This chapter has described the core of the SENCO's work which is:

- The maintenance of paperwork and organisation of review procedures associated with the Code of Practice register.
- The monitoring of IEPs and associated curriculum planning and assessment for all pupils with SEN.

The prime aim of all of these tasks is to improve the opportunities for pupils with SEN to learn effectively, access the curriculum, make progress and be valued and full members of the school community. The SENCO will make this happen if they can both organise efficiently and work in a supportive way with all concerned. This consultative role will be considered in the next chapter.

CHAPTER 9

Supporting Others: the Consultancy Role

The role of SENCO requires an ability to work with colleagues, pupils, parents as well as other professionals. Much of this work is of a consultative nature. Everyone looks to the SENCO for support, advice and even counselling. How much of this, rather less formal, work any particular SENCO can do, depends on a number of factors. The first of these factors is the SENCO's own feeling of confidence. This will be stronger when based on a feeling of competence built up through knowledge and skills gained from experience. It takes time, often many years, to build up this confidence and competence, so as to be in a position to support others and act as a change agent in a school. During these years, when experience is being gained, training is also necessary to acquire the knowledge and skills to carry out the job to the full.

The second of the factors which will enhance and facilitate the consultative role, is the school's general policies and ethos. It will matter how, for example, parents are perceived as part of the school community. Is there an honest, open attitude towards partnership with parents? Are parents' views welcomed and considered when policies are being developed? Are pupils' perspectives valued in the way policies and procedures for the whole population in the school have been developed? Are staff valued and given praise by senior management? The needs of teachers have to be met if they in turn are to meet the needs of children, especially those children who are more difficult to teach.

Galloway (1985) defined children with special needs as those children that caused teachers stress, either because they couldn't learn and make progress as expected, or because they could not conform to the norms of behaviour expected by the teacher. If the school is set up to support staff and give them ways of dealing with stressful situations collaboratively, the role of the SENCO will be a more effective part of this process. Where the school is not as supportive to teachers, pupils or parents as it should be, the consultative role for the SENCO will be much harder. He or she will have to choose those parts of the 'system' which can be worked with to achieve some success. The consultative role will have to begin with small actions wherever possible. This is in order to preserve the SENCO's own health and ability to cope with what is already a very complex job. The golden rule for SENCOs, where things are difficult in some way, are to remember that:

- Small is beautiful.
- Work with the healthy parts of the system.

In other words, it is better to find one colleague who can be positively supported and help gain confidence and competence, than to try to do too much too fast. Don't expect too much change to occur too quickly. Where the system is more developed and there are already many positive features, such as colleagues who have gained competence in meeting individual needs, working with parents and working collaboratively with others, then the scale of what can be achieved will be bigger and the rate of change faster.

This chapter looks at three aspects of the SENCO's consultative role:

- Working with pupils: considering pupil perspectives and rights.
- Working in partnership with parents: dealing with stress and complaints.
- Working with colleagues: giving support and training.

Each section will look both at the personal skills of the SENCO and features of the whole-school approach, which together contribute to effective development of the consultative role.

Enhancing pupil perspectives

To achieve an understanding of the pupil's own view of their school experience and their educational needs requires an ability on the part of the teacher to change perspective. Teachers have to let go of their position of authority, for a short time, and view the world of the classroom from the pupil's point of view. This may best be done through becoming a careful observer for certain times. If someone else can manage the class for a short session while this observation takes place, it may be easier to observe.

Observation impartiality

Accurate observation for as little as ten minutes, if focused and prepared, can give some insights into a particular area of concern, whether an individual pupil or a group. Always remember that observation will be affected by bias, so if more than one adult can observe to a prepared schedule, the results may be more reliable.

Observation skills

Learning observation skills gives teachers a useful tool for assessment and general problem-solving. Observations can be for set times (ten minutes) or of specific events or of a specific context, such as the playground. Starting the observation without a precise focus may be possible, but increasingly focusing in on an intended feature may give more insight. If pupil perspectives are the focus, this may need to be combined with interview techniques. There are a number of observation techniques given in Appendix 9a.

Interviews

Another way to get a pupil's perspective is, of course, to ask the pupil to talk about or express their views in some way. This can be by direct questions about an aspect of their work, such as reading or homework, or it can be more open-ended questioning about school, friends, events etc. Open-ended interviewing is difficult for some teachers to do, partly because of time constraints. Sometimes other adults, ancillary helpers or support professionals may fare better, because they may offer less threat to pupils, or have time to see pupils in a more relaxed environment.

Questionnaires

The whole class can be given exercises to evaluate an aspect of their own learning; to give ratings about how confident they feel about various aspects of their learning. For younger pupils, faces with different expressions can be used to rate answers instead of words (See example Appendix 9b).

Triangulation

It is more difficult to gain a view of pupil perspective where the pupil lacks the language to express their thoughts and feelings in words. In these cases observations from more than one adult may need to be combined to giving a feel for the pupil's perspective. Ancillary helpers' and parents' observations about different aspects of the pupil's development and feelings of self-worth, are very helpful in putting together a joint perspective. If video cameras and tape recorders are used, this can help collect valuable data in cases where more direct questioning is difficult, for example, the developmentally young or pupils with language impairment. These would not be kept as a long-term record, but might help analyse complex observations.

Symbolic representation

Drawings and symbolic representations of situations as perceived during play can all add to the teacher's understanding of pupil perspectives.

Learning observation and interview techniques

All of the above takes time, just for one child, and will not be possible to do for all the pupils in a class or on the SEN register. Different methods can be selected for different children and at different times. It is useful however if, as part of training sessions, teachers can practice some of the skills required in collecting and collating information which will enhance their ability to look at pupil perspectives. For some teachers the exercise of *really* trying to understand one pupil, from a child's point of view, is a revelation and may later affect attitudes when working with other pupils (see Appendices 9a and b).

School policy taking pupil perspectives into account

The Code of Practice emphasises the benefits of involving the child in assessment and intervention. These benefits are:

- Practical – children have important and relevant information. Their support is crucial to the effective implementation of any individual education programme.
- Principle – children have a right to be heard. They should be encouraged to participate in decision-making about provision to meet their special educational needs. Code of Practice, Par 2.35

Schools should make every attempt to identify the views and wishes of the child or young person and consider how the school will:

> - Involve pupils in decision-making processes.
> - Determine the pupil's level of participation, taking into account approaches to assessment and intervention which are suitable for his or her age, ability and past experiences.
> - Record pupil's views in identifying their difficulties, setting goals, agreeing a development strategy, monitoring and reviewing progress.
> - Involve pupils in implementing individual education plans.
>
> Code of Practice, Par 2.37

It will help if the school develops procedures for regularly taking note of pupil perspectives. For example, Individual Education Plan proformas need to have a space to note pupil's views (see Appendix 3b). Regular conferencing times when pupil's views are taken down, can be built into the review procedure for IEPs. The Records of Achievement approach to recording progress, as part of the school's assessment policy, will enhance the work for those working in special needs.

As part of the review of the SEN policy, these questions need to be asked:

- Do we take account of pupil viewpoints and perspectives?
- Do we have procedures and times when we can note pupil viewpoints and perspectives?
- Do pupil views and perspectives influence policy making in the school?

Opinions will vary, of course, amongst staff as to whether pupil's views should be given any priority. Some staff may even disagree fundamentally with the principle of listening to pupils. In such situations the golden rules of 'small is beautiful' and 'working with the positive parts of the system' will need to be kept in mind. SENCOs, of all people on the staff, do, at least for themselves, need to keep the pupil perspective in mind when planning for individuals with SEN. In conclusion, it is worth considering the focus of the 1989 Children Act. As Garner and Sandow (1995) state, 'The 1989 Children Act represents the first serious attempt to include views of children in any decisions about their welfare.' (p. 11) However, as they go on to discuss, children seem to have far fewer rights in schools. They conclude that: 'The whole issue of the rights of children is subordinated to the rights of parents and of the educational establishments, to make decisions on their behalf.' (p.3)

Their book on *Advocacy, Self Advocacy and Special Needs* goes on to discuss self advocacy as a human right, particularly for those children with emotional and behavioural difficulties or severe learning difficulties and is recommended to those who wish to read more about the issues concerning pupil perspectives in SEN.

Working in partnership with parents

Just as understanding the pupils' viewpoints needed a change of perspective for the teacher, so often does understanding the parents' viewpoint. If a true partnership with parents' to be established, then the teacher or the SENCO needs to learn to listen to and value the parents' expertise about their own child or their concerns about his or her progress.

To do this effectively, it is necessary to learn new skills. Teachers are good at expressing themselves and activating ideas. They may not be quite as good as listeners. Listening effectively in the consultative role is a skill to be learnt and practised. A head commented that possibly teacher appraisals may be increasing awareness of the importance of listening carefully to others.

Empathic listening

In this mode the listener obeys certain ground rules. These are:

- Keep eye contact.
- Keep still, do not distract your listener by fiddling with pens etc.
- Keep your own comments to a minimum, such as 'I see', 'Right', 'I understand' and 'Yes' etc.
- If longer comments are required, make these reflective, i.e. feedback the main point as you understood it, so it can be checked. Use these comments to summarise the points and check you have understood what was said.
- Don't be afraid to feed back feelings as well as facts. 'That must have made you angry', 'You were upset by ...'.

Such listening sessions will need time limits, so these should be set up in advance if possible – 'We've got half an hour – please tell me your concerns, worries ... and we will try to find some answers to the problems'. Check that the parent is happy for you to take notes. Often it is not a good idea to do this, if you are really trying to listen. You cannot keep eye contact and write notes. It may be a good idea to make time to summarise at the end of the session and agree a few points which can be written down. Establishing a feeling of trust is more important than note taking at this point. Once the problem has been identified and the parent feels they were listened to, it is possible to move into a *problem-solving mode*.

Problem solving

As a first step, this requires that the problem has been clearly identified. Next, actions can be jointly planned with the parent to try to solve the problem. Problem solving again needs a sensitive approach from the teacher, while setting boundaries for what is achievable in school within limited resources. Wherever possible, the parents will feel more of a partner if they can suggest ideas to be discussed, perhaps offer to help in some way at home or in school. Joint targets can then be set and a date to review progress made. Copies of written notes of meetings should be given to parents wherever possible.

Parents' rights and involvement

Parents are defined under the Children Act (1989) as those who have parental responsibility for the child or who have care of the child (full description in Appendix 9c). Over the last two decades, legislation has increased parents' rights in relation to schools, choices and information as is shown in the summary of Education Acts given below.

Summary of Education Acts in relation to parents rights

Education Acts since 1980 have given increasing rights to all parents. The 1981 and 1993 Act gave rights to parents of pupils with SEN.

1980 Education Act

In this legislation, parents, other than those whose child had a statement, were granted the right to choose the school they wished to send their children to. Parents were also given the right to be represented on the governing bodies of schools (Hornby, p.88).

1981 Education Act

Parents involvement in the formal assessment of their child increased under this Act. Parents also were given the right to appeal first to the LEA and then to the Secretary of State about decisions made by the LEA, as a result of making a multi-professional assessment for a statement.

1986 Education Act

The first of two Education Acts passed in 1986 required increased parental representation on the governing bodies of schools. Governors were required to present an annual report to parents and to have a meeting with parents at the school in order to discuss the report (Hornby, p.89).

1988 Education Act

This Act granted parents the right to send their children to any school of their choice so long as it has room for them. It also required that parents are sent an annual report on their children's progress. In addition, it gave schools the opportunity of opting out of LEA control if a majority of parents voted in favour of this (Hornby, p.89).

1992 Education Act

It was this Act that set out the new inspection procedures for schools. Teams of independent inspectors co-ordinated by the Office for Standards in Education (OFSTED) were to inspect all maintained schools. Parents had a right to meet the inspectors before the inspection to discuss any issue they wished which could include how the needs pupils with SEN were met and how parents were involved in reviews.

1993 Education Act

This Act gave an important change of emphasis to parental rights. The SEN Tribunal gave the parents right of appeal against LEA decisions related to assessment (see other sections of this chapter). The Act also promised the Code of Practice which emphasises parents' rights through partnership (see 'Schools' arrangements for parents', on p.94). This legislation obliged schools to develop policies to implement partnership arrangements:

Schedule 1:15

> The School's policy should contain a clear statement of the school's arrangements for ensuring close working partnership with parents of children with special educational needs. Those arrangements should be drawn up having regard to the Code of Practice, in particular paragraphs 2:28–2:33, and cover such matters as arrangements for recording and acting upon parental concern; procedures for involving parents when a concern is first expressed within the school; arrangements for incorporating parents' views in assessment and subsequent reviews; and arrangements for ensuring that parents are fully informed about the school's procedures and are made welcome in the school. Circular 6/94 Par 52

Schools' arrangements for parents

The Code of Practice states that:

> - A school's arrangements for parents of children with special educational needs should include:
> - Information on the school's SEN policy;
> - on the support available for children with special educational needs within the school and LEA;
> - on parents' involvement in assessment and decision-making, emphasising the importance of their contributions;
> - on services such as those provided by the local authority for children 'in need';
> - on local and national voluntary organisations which might provide information, advice or counselling;
> - arrangements for recording and acting upon parental concern;
> - procedures for involving parents when a concern is first expressed within the school;
> - arrangements for incorporating parents' views in assessment and subsequent reviews;
> - access for parents;
> - information in a range of community languages;
> - information on tape for parents who may have literacy or communication difficulties;
> - a parents' room or other arrangements in the school to help parents feel confident and comfortable. (Code of Practice Par 2.33)

Much of this will be achieved if a policy for parents of all pupils is inclusive and enhances participation. SEN policy should not be an add-on but an integral part of the school's general way of working with parents. Mallett (1995) suggests that the following might be ways of doing this:

- Explaining the school's staged approach to meeting SEN, at a parents' meeting.
- Holding a 'hands on' differentiation 'workshop,' so that parents, teachers and classroom assistants can share making the curriculum accessible.

But certainly involving parents in the monitoring and evaluating of the school's performance relating to the targets set for the SEN policy is essential (**see also Activity 6**).

If schools have listened to parents when developing other policies, then parents' perspectives will already be reflected. Parents of pupils with SEN are however, particularly vulnerable. Parents of children with difficulties and disabilities may lack confidence themselves, may even feel guilty (unjustifiably), about their child. Such parents are not always confident enough to ask for their views to be taken into account or to even know their rights. It is therefore essential that the SENCO gives parents information about these rights to be listened to. Parents need to have the five-staged assessment procedure explained. They need to know about LEA services which may be called on to support their child. School provision for SEN needs to be explained also.

There are a few parents however who seem to have all too much confidence and knowledge of their rights. Such parents can pose a threat to some teachers and the SENCO in particular. To make a partnership with these parents requires skills of assertiveness and ability to set limits, in particular:

- Knowing how to say 'no'.
- Knowing how to limit time spent.

Such parents can be aggressive, even rude. Their feelings of anger, guilt and frustration over finding their child is not making expected progress can be let loose on an unsuspecting and caring SENCO, with the result that instead of a partnership, a confrontation occurs. As Dale (1996) explains, parents can go through a 'psychic shock' when they first hear of their child's disability. The first phase may only last a day or so, at which time they need sympathy and understanding. After that their need is for information to help them orientate better. The next step will be to use a problem-solving approach to help parents come to terms with the new situation. This situation is of course best avoided by preventative strategies. Empathic listening can still help establish a rapport followed by a structured problem solving session. If the parent feels they really have been listened to and their view points taken into account, they may be able to calm down and look for joint practical solutions.

If, however, their feelings seem irrational and solutions are beyond the resources of the school, it may be necessary to get help either from other members of the school, the head, for example, or outside professionals (see **Source List 2** for further reading).

Almost all parents can be brought into a partnership situation even if only in small ways. Difficulties arise when promises are broken, resources lent don't come back to school, the pupil is absent intermittently or for long periods. In many of these cases the teacher's motivation to work positively dwindles and possibly so does the parent's. It is sometimes difficult to keep the child's interests central to the problem solution. The parents' needs can only be addressed by the teacher insofar as they affect the pupil. Parents' own adult needs cannot be addressed by the school, although it is possible sometimes to get a personal referral for help.

The questions SENCOs need to keep in mind when working with parents are:

- What is a possible outcome of this meeting which will benefit the child in question?
- What resources are available from the school, or the community, to support this child and parent?
- What is achievable in the immediate future and in the more distant future?

Being able to summarise the answers to these questions and feed back to the parent in a positive manner will be a way of recording the meeting.

Dealing with complaints

Schedule 1:12 states that the school SEN policy must include a section on how complaints will be dealt with:

> The policy should make clear to parents of children with SEN how they can make a complaint about the provision made for their child at the school and how that complaint will subsequently be dealt with by the school. Such information could include the time targets in which the school aims to respond. Circular 6/94 Par 49

Schools usually have a general complaints system, but will need to give particular attention to SEN complaints. Often it is to the class teacher or the SENCO that the parent first turns. If the matter can be dealt with easily and quietly, this is best. It should be kept clearly in mind that the head teacher has the final responsibility for the school along with the governors. It is important therefore that procedures are clearly set out and published and not left to chance.

The SEN Tribunal (See also Chapter 8)

The SEN tribunal was set up by the Education Act 1993. It considers parents' appeals against decisions of the LEA about a child's special educational needs where the parents cannot reach agreement with the LEA. *SEN tribunals, How to appeal*, DfE 1994c. states that parents have the right to appeal to the SEN tribunal if:

- They disagree with the LEA's decision not to assess and they, the parents, have been involved in requesting that assessment. Code of Practice, Par 3:96
- After making a statutory assessment, the LEA does not issue a statement but issues a 'note in lieu'. Code of Practice, Par 4:17
- They disagree with the content of Part 2 of the final statement or final amended statement (description of child's SEN), Part 3 (Description of special educational provision), Part 4 (name of school). Code of Practice, Par 4:68, 4:69
- The LEA refuses to reassess the child's SEN and the parents' request was made more that 6 months after any previous assessment. Code of Practice, Par 6:40
- Named changes of school (e.g. at phase changes 6:32)
- LEA not naming a school. Code of Practice, Par 6:33
- Disagree with LEA's decision not to maintain a statement. Par 6.36.

Parents *cannot* use the SEN tribunal to complain about the way the LEA are carrying out an assessment, providing help as stated, or the way the school is meeting their child's SEN, nor can they use this to appeal against the description of non-educational provision in the statement.

LEA must give parents all the information available about their right to appeal, including a free copy of the parents leaflet on *How to Appeal*. They also should put the parents in touch with voluntary organisations or the parent partnership officer who will support them in their appeal. The LEA should also have offered the parents a named person during the assessment procedure.

The first appeals to the tribunal began in mid January 1995. Although the intention was not to make them confrontational or to populate them with lawyers, this has often been the case. Parents do not need to be represented by a lawyer, but many have chosen to do so, although legal aid is only available for preparation not presentation of the case. As Garner and Sandow (1995) comment, 'We need to wait and see whether tribunals will operate smoothly and if parents from all sections of the community will feel able to use them'. (p. 124)

Parents from one group, namely those whose children are dyslexic, have to date, taken up over 40 per cent of the tribunal's time. These parents have used a consumer led model, demanding considerable resources from the SEN budget to meet what they consider to be the only solution to their child's problem. As Garner and Sandow suggest:

> They therefore successfully subvert the system by directing SEN budgets away from most children. If all parents were taking such a consumer role, the results could well be confrontation rather than collaboration.
>
> p.125

The tribunal process is very stressful for parents and takes a long time. It is not clear that it benefits the child to any great extent. It is clearly much better to try to reach agreement with parents and to work in partnership in coming to these agreements. As Gascoigne (1995) says:

> The best strategy for dealing with complaints is to prevent them. The most effective strategy is to develop partnership with parents, on an individual basis, school basis and authority basis; through developing links with local and national voluntary organisations and parent support groups.
>
> p.147

Supporting colleagues

Much of what has been said in the previous sections applies to working successfully with colleagues. They too need someone to share concerns, so listening skills will apply here as will problem solving strategies. Often colleagues only need to be reassured that they are doing the right thing. Being able to describe their problem, express their concerns and anxieties will be sufficient to produce the feeling of being supported. It may be wise to follow this up by observation of the child or group in question. Fuller assessment may be part of the solution. Interview with pupil and parents may be indicated.

It is not the SENCO's role to know all answers to all questions. What they can do is to facilitate the **problem solving abilities** of their colleagues and help them find solutions which they feel will work. These solutions may require the SENCO to work collaboratively with the class or child, or they may be to request precise advice on strategies on resources. Being able to enter into productive dialogues with colleagues is **the skill** the SENCO will need to develop most. It is, of course, more likely that the SENCO will also have knowledge of a particular strategy or resource to help a particular child if they have experience of a wide range of SEN themselves or have access to specialist advice (see Chapters 6 and 7).

The SENCO's role in supporting in-service training for SEN

Schedule 1:13

> The school's policy should, in accordance with the Code of Practice, describe plans for the in-service training and professional development of staff. Where appropriate, the school's in-service training policy should cover the needs of non-teaching assistants. In drawing up their policies, the school should inform itself of the LEA's in-service training policy and consider both the training needs of the SEN co-ordinator and how he or she can be equipped to provide training for fellow teachers. The school's policy should also set out any joint arrangements with other schools. (Circular 6/94, Par 50)

It is often seen as part of the SENCO's role to take the lead in in-service sessions on the various aspects of SEN. Just how feasible this is again depends on the existing knowledge and competence level of the SENCO him/herself. Many aspects of SEN policy and procedures can be dealt with in-house by the SENCO. It needs to be recognised however, that the more specialist areas may not be known by anyone in one school and it is then that help needs to be bought in from outside services or professionals. For example, if a pupil with a rare disability is about to be integrated, the specialist teacher or other professional may be the best person to run an in-service session.

This book has been an attempt to enskill SENCOs with knowledge and ideas which they can use to support and train their colleagues. Each chapter had within it both factual and theoretical information about what must be done to meet the requirements of the 1993 Act and the Code of Practice, as well as practical suggestions for implementation. The chapters, together with appendices and source lists and activity pack, should help SENCOs to fulfil their role as trainer and supporter of their colleagues.

CHAPTER 10

The Role of the SENCO: Working within a Whole-school Approach

The purpose of this final chapter is to examine the SEN co-ordinator's role in its totality within the context of whole-school development. Schools are being challenged to become more effective, more independent of LEA support and at the same time to enter a competitive market for pupils. Standards are continually being deplored in the media, seldom praised and the pressure grows to produce good public examination or standard assessment task results. However, for those pupils with a wide range of difficulties or disabilities, who are successfully included within the mainstream population, outcome measures are less easily judged.

Schools are being asked to be more efficient in managing resources, and to improve the quality of teaching and learning for *all* pupils. One characteristic of a good school is that it has established good management of resources which maximise the potential effectiveness of the whole institution. This must include the allocation of resources to meet SEN which must be clearly defined and understood by parents. (The issue of how LEAs devolve funds to schools under LMS arrangements lies outside the scope of this book, but Lunt and Evans (1994) explore this in depth.) How does the special needs child fare in all of this? Are they a 'kid with a price tag', bringing the resource of a statement, or are they to be welcomed as part of a diverse community and valued for their contribution and achievements? A successful inclusion policy is far more to do with attitudes than money and developing effective inclusive education remains a challenge which the majority of schools wish to meet. 'society is made up of other peoples' children' was a remark frequently made by Joan Sallis when talking to my course members. By this she meant that we cannot afford to educate only the high achievers or the easy-to-teach children, because every child will be part of our future.

Inclusive education

Rieser (1995), writing from the viewpoint of the Disabled People's movement, proposes that SEN should be part of an equal opportunities policy and not treated as a separate issue. He points out that 'the focus on the individual child rather than the whole curriculum and how it needs to change, has led to isolation, exclusion, separation, and sometimes compulsory segregation', (p 40).

He explains that the medical model, which typifies so much SEN work, results in seeing the disabled person as having a problem which needs treatment. (The term disabled is here interpreted as including all those with impairments or chronic illnesses, as well as those with any learning or emotional or behavioural difficulty.) The social model, on the other hand, recognises that disabled people may have a wide range of impairments with varying loss of function, but proposes that it is the limitations of opportunities which creates disability. This is due to physical, social or attitudinal barriers. Adopting a social model of SEN, within a whole-school approach, will mean thinking of ways to break down such barriers. Some of this will mean returning to policies against bullying, for example, and addressing name-calling, using negative descriptions of body and mind; or reviewing the behaviour policy to include the inculcation of attitudes of mutual respect and strong equality principles. As one head remarked, 'we need a policy to help make and review policies!' Any successful policy which allows pupils to express their thoughts and feelings with confidence in a climate of trust, will benefit everyone.

Evaluating SEN as an issue within whole-school development

Schools need a process for evaluating their policies and choosing yearly priorities for development Russell (1994) says that the most innovative features of the Code of Practice are its staged approach to assessment and its recognition that clarity about roles and responsibilities for children with SEN needs to be established. She thought that 'requiring schools to have SEN policies should have a very powerful impact on the quality and coherence of provision for special needs within the mainstream sector', (p.48).

Many schools have begun formulating their SEN polices by writing down existing procedures and practice under the 17 headings required by Schedule 1. While this has made a start and satisfied minimum requirements of the Code of Practice, to make the policy dynamic will require further work. A first step will be to examine the value systems and determine the principles underlying policies.

Russell (1995a) suggests a possible principle as being 'one of increasing and maintaining the participation of pupils with a range of SEN and other problems within the educational and social life of the community', (p.70). Some schools will need to start further back because their values and philosophies may not be so clear.

Schools will need to collate information about how they use specialist resources to support pupils with SEN; how they work with parents as partners and how they celebrate diversity. She suggests that this may require disability equality training opportunities for teachers, governors, parents and pupils.

Frederickson (1993) puts forward the use of Soft Systems Methodology (SSM) to help identify and solve problems which are intrinsically complex and messy like those of SEN. SSM is a semi-structured systems method of identifying and analysing an organisation issue. Using this can 'suspend preconceptions and allow a range of possible purposes to be logically worked through: future scenarios constructed, their implications identified and their cultural feasibility openly debated.' (Frederickson, 1993, p.17)

This type of systems thinking was successfully used as the methodology underlying the school-focused projects carried out by SENIOS course members training to be SEN Co-ordinators. They found two elements of the method particularly useful in deciding on priority areas for their school's development. The first was drawing the 'rich picture' diagram pulling in all information available in a schematic and evocative format. After examining this, teachers could visualise the social and political systems surrounding their work. They became aware, for example, of informal as well as formal power structures within the school.

The second element was the recognition which SSM raised of the 'world view' and outside constraints which impinged on their work. Both internal and external influences constrained what transformations were possible; providing boundaries to choosing changes which would be feasible, efficient and effective. Future action plans then become clearer.

Evaluation of the SENCO role

Reviewing policy will include reviewing the tasks required by the SENCO along with other roles and responsibilities. The workload of SENCOs has increased dramatically since the Code of Practice. But long before 1994 the demands were growing. Pressures came from the wish to include a wider range of pupils, which led in turn to more support systems to manage. A debate around the role of SEN co-ordinators was led by Dyson in his 1990 paper in which he wrote 'Special needs co-ordinators are a dying breed. In ten years time they will be as out of date as remedial teachers or special classes are today' (p.116). His argument in this and his 1991 paper hinges on the paradoxical nature of the role. He found many SENCOs saw conflict between their work as specialist teachers, supporting a minority of pupils, and the whole-school approach. If specialist expertise was thus dissipated, there might not be any justification for the role because it diverted resources away from the ordinary work of the school.

By 1994, the role of the SENCO had been written into the Code of Practice thus legitimising its existence and increasing the workload on those who held the posts. Tensions still exist between wishing to use time to support pupils, parents and colleagues (the consultative role) and dealing with ever-increasing paperwork (the co-ordinating role), (see Chapters 8 and 9). The most significant dilemma which arises directly from the Code of Practice is the drive it produces towards individualising support and resources in contrast to diversifying resources to support a differentiated curriculum for all. The IEP becomes the focal point of this dilemma (see Chapters 3, 4 and 5).

Dyson picks up the thread again in his 1995 paper and links it to the conflicts within the different constructs of special needs which arise from his view of a whole-school approach. He points out that managing a whole-school policy is not a technical task of an organisational or routine nature but about 'managing a process of construction which is characterised by evidence of conflict'. (Dyson 1995, p.64). His solutions lie in establishing broad principles of debate, boundaries and power, implying that the **head teacher** has the responsibility for special needs provision and should manage this as part of the school's activities with suitable management structures in place. The SENCO becomes **an effective learning consultant.**

Special Educational Needs as a construct

Everyone builds up their own construct of special needs from their experience and knowledge, both personal and professional. My own research (Cowne, 1993) demonstrated how this construct developed for course members as a result of attending SENIOS courses and working on school-based action research projects. SENCOs and special needs teachers built up their confidence and competence by learning both the theory and practice of individual assessment and teaching; curriculum planning and differentiation; effective classroom management techniques and consultancy skills. This construct grew in complexity as the teachers gained more experience and reflected on their own learning. The construct was not fixed, each individual had a core which was personal to them. It follows that the SENCO's role will also be built up from an interaction between the individual's constructs and those of significant numbers of the school's staff. Each school builds its value systems, out of which all the policies, priorities and roles develop.

But it is only when SENCOs are supported by heads or what one head called 'a critical number' (he suggested three staff), that change in the institution can occur, Head teachers' constructs of SEN differed including much more about resource issues, or where advice could be found or how staff development could occur. They saw SEN policy as helping to develop good classroom management and well-planned curriculum differentiation. This would result in better standards of teaching in their schools. SEN development, therefore, became a lever for other school development and their SENCOs were often perceived as agents of change. It must be recalled that this group were SENCOs who had experienced the learning from the SENIOS courses, and who had become **effective teacher researchers**.

O'Hanlon (1993) confirms my findings that qualitative practitioner research provides the foundation for individual and institutional change. She says that 'critical enquiry within the school empowers the teacher researcher, and it allows the special needs teacher to share evidence, discuss issues and engage in reflective decision-making with colleagues.' (p. 103).

She comments that special needs work is often carried out in 'occupied territory' and the role requires 'barter, negotiation and compromise.' It is complex and emotive, but she argues that conflict is the very centre of institutional change and can be resolved as long as communication is maintained. Her view is of a change agent who works as a reflective practitioner to address these change issues and help resolve the tensions. This confirms my own findings that by engaging in reflective conversations, the SENCO can act as **an agent of change**.

Scope of this book

This book has attempted to give both practical advice and theoretical background to support SEN policy development and the SEN Co-ordinator's role within that development. Some readers will be experienced and for them I hope to have stimulated thought and challenged them to further reading. Others will have been more recently appointed and will need some of the detail the book provides. But this book does not have all the answers. Some questions require local knowledge; some further reading. The Code of Practice will need careful examining for detail not provided here. Ramjhun (1995) adds further guidance to the Code's interpretation. The National Children's Bureau, SENJIT and Institute of Education's SEN Policy Pack (1995), quoted frequently in this book, will be an additional source for staff development exercises. This book has tried to show SEN issues as part of a wider process of developing effective inclusive education. SENCOs may not all do identical tasks, as every school will find ways of sharing the work between staff, according to differences of size, phase or philosophy. SENCOs may acquire new labels such as those suggested in this chapter. They will have a significant role to play as long as they remain reflective practitioners, able to manage change in themselves, and hold meaningful conversations with colleagues and parents, to develop the expertise and attitudes to make ordinary schools special places for all pupils.

WSPSEN
Activity Pack

Whole-School Policy for
Special Educational Needs

1. Roles and Responsibilities: exercise

2. Audit of Whole-school Policy

3. Lesson Planning for Differentiation

4. Room Management: exercise

5. Information Flow for IEPs: exercise

6. Reviewing Parental Policy

WSPSEN
Activity Pack

Activity One: Roles and Responsibilities for SEN

Step 1. List tasks which are seen as essential for your school in relation to the maintenance and management of your WSPSEN.

Step 2. List people who will be involved in these tasks at:
   A = Action Level; S = Strategic Level; I = Need for Information Level.

Step 3. Using grid (see model), write in tasks and names/roles of people.

Step 4. Discussion of the grid in groups to reach concensus on levels A, S & I for each task and role.

Step 5. Draw up an action plan in relation to roles and responsibilities. Check:
- Whose role is going to change significantly?
- How will all staff be informed?
- How much time will be needed by individuals with Action roles?
- How will this be achieved?
- How will information flow between A & S & I roles?

Step 6: Discuss evaluation criteria and timing:
- When will this plan be evaluated?
- Who will be asked for their views?

Set review date and write main points into your WSPSEN.

WSPSEN - Activity Pack

Activity One: Model for Roles and Responsibilities Activity in WSPSEN

Examples→ People Tasks ↓	Class Teacher	SENCO/ Support Staff	Year Head or Deputy	Head	Governor
Identify & assess pupils with SEN (stage 1)					
Maintain SEN Register					
Write IEPs for Stage 2 Stage 3 Stage 4					
Differentiate Curriculum					
Resource Curriculum Modifications					
Monitor pupil progress and organise review procedures					
Manage support staff					
Liaise with outside agencies					
Liaise/work with parents					
Inform Governors of changes					

WSPSEN
Activity Pack

Activity Two:
Reviewing your whole-school policy for special educational needs

Notes to SENCO

This exercise does several things. It gives opportunities for staff to reflect on what should be in your policy and how it is working at present. It gives an opportunity for groups to discuss their priorities after personal reflection and to justify their point of view to colleagues. It gives the steering group or the SENCO an opportunity to see what staff really think is happening. It may reveal gaps in their knowledge or it may show very strong differences of opinion. These can be further explored in the discussion groups. Although this exercise has proved to be most useful in a half day's in-service, it can be given out as a 'questionnaire' to staff prior to a staff meeting and the outcomes of the analysis discussed in a shorter meeting later. The statements must *not* be phrased as questions but must remain statements. **Its main purpose is as a vehicle for discussion** rather than to be heavily analysed. However, the analysis can give information to the steering group, which may inform staff development needs.

How to use the sample statement sheets

This exercise covers all aspects of a whole-school policy. Add or remove items to suit your school's priorities. It allows staff to reflect on the various aspects of the policy and gives a base-line to the SENCO for further work.

Below are a list of statements covering various aspects of the whole-school policy for SEN. Under each statement are two lines marked a) and b) with a numbered scale from 1-5.

The staff members are given the list. For each statement, each member is asked to ring the number which indicates the extent to which this statement **ought** to be a principle on which the policy is based - this is working from **belief**. And the staff member also rings a number which indicates the extent to which the statement describes the policy **as implemented to date** - this is working from **reality**. After this is done, individuals break into small groups, such as year or curriculum teams, to reach some consensus of opinion on the most important priorities for the next year's work on the policy. This group activity starts by collating the group's individual results and looking for the biggest/smallest gap between the upper and lower line of markings.

WSPSEN
Activity Pack

Activity Two Checklist: how to use it

This checklist contains 15 statements about SEN policy or arrangements in schools. Its purpose is to help identify those points of your school's policy or arrangements in which there is scope for improvement. Each statement is followed by two lines a) and b) for rating on a scale 1-5.

Line a) Ring the number which represents the extent to which this **ought** to be in the whole school policy on SEN.
1 = must not be in; 5 = must be in.

Line b) Ring the number which represents your view of the **actual** situation at present.
1 = not happening at all; 5 = happening completely.

If you wish, two more statements can be added to cover any aspects not already mentioned. Rank these is the same way as the others.

The difference between the ratings of the two lines may indicate the school's most important areas for action on the policy development. Discussion following this exercise within a staff or in-service meeting will serve as a way to reach consensus over priorities for the next year. (Concept developed from Evans *et al*, 1981).

Activity Two: Checklist

1. There is an operational policy for SEN which has principles consistent with the Code of Practice.
   a) 1   2   3   4   5
   b) 1   2   3   4   5

2. The key principles of this policy are known to staff and inform the school's provision for pupils with SEN.
   a) 1   2   3   4   5
   b) 1   2   3   4   5

3. There are descriptive guidelines of the roles and responsibilities of staff for SEN. These include roles for governors, head, SENCO and all staff.
   a) 1   2   3   4   5
   b) 1   2   3   4   5

4. All staff are aware of the procedures used to identify, access and record the needs of pupils with SEN.
   a) 1   2   3   4   5
   b) 1   2   3   4   5

5. There are arrangements in place to organise regular reviews of progress for all pupils with SEN.
   a) 1   2   3   4   5
   b) 1   2   3   4   5

6. Pupils are supported in understanding the assessment and provision for their SEN and are involved in the decision-making during planning the IEPs.
    a) 1   2   3   4   5
    b) 1   2   3   4   5

7. Staff are supported in the development of a range of teaching strategies, learning activities and support materials which enhance the access to the curriculum for pupils with SEN.
    a) 1   2   3   4   5
    b) 1   2   3   4   5

8. Individual planning for pupils with SEN is an integral part of general curriculum planning.
    a) 1   2   3   4   5
    b) 1   2   3   4   5

9. There is a staff development policy for SEN which relates to the school development plan and reflects individual staff priorities and needs.
    a) 1   2   3   4   5
    b) 1   2   3   4   5

10. Parents are kept informed of their child's SEN and are involved in the planning of future targets for their child.
    a) 1   2   3   4   5
    b) 1   2   3   4   5

11. Parents are given information about the school's policy and procedures for SEN. A positive whole-school partnership is encouraged.
    a) 1   2   3   4   5
    b) 1   2   3   4   5

12. School and support staff work in a flexible way to enhance full pupil integration.
    a) 1   2   3   4   5
    b) 1   2   3   4   5

13. Liaison time is available for class and subject teachers to plan effective use of support time.
    a) 1   2   3   4   5
    b) 1   2   3   4   5

14. The school's allocation of resources for SEN reflects various levels of need for different groups of pupils and the need to draw on outside support services and agencies for some.
    a) 1   2   3   4   5
    b) 1   2   3   4   5

15. There is a mechanism in place for monitoring and evaluating the SEN policy in practice.
    a) 1   2   3   4   5
    b) 1   2   3   4   5

WSPSEN
Activity Pack

Activity Three: Lesson Plan for Differentiation

1. Choose a topic within your subject.

2. Answer questions 1 & 2.

3. Define core objectives for the lesson.

    What should the pupils learn? (Give range of outcomes if necessary).

4. What assessment modalities (oral, written, demonstration, product) will be used?

5. Write down pre-requisite baseline skills or concepts that you are assuming to be present in the class, before you start. (Change boxes to suit yourself).

6. Introduce fully-written IEPs for SEN pupils.

7. Decide if any modifications to your planning are necessary in the light of the IEPs.

8. Add extension ideas for your more able pupils or the whole class.

9. If staff development time allows, discuss continuity and cross-curricular issues. What should have been covered by previous lessons or other subjects? Will this cause confusion to students? Are there 'bridging' needs to cross reference between subjects?

WSPSEN - Activity Pack
Activity Three

Differentiation Exercise for Key Stage 1 & 2 lessons

Question 1 Is this realistic to do in the time allocated?		Question 2 Is this relevant to this group of students?
Modification	Topic	
	Core curriculum objectives	
	Strategies/methods/resources	Extension
	Assessment modality	

Pre-requisite baseline skills

Language Skills (oral)	Language (written)	Social skills	Key concepts needed
Manipulative	Number skills	Organisational skills	

WSPSEN - Activity Pack
Activity Three

Differentation exercise for a Key Stage 3 lesson

Question 1 Is this realistic to do in the time allocated?		Question 2 Is this relevant to this group of students?
	Topic	
	Core curriculum objectives e.g Tasks - Skills - Concepts	
Modification for SEN	Delivery method/resource	**Extension**
	Assessment modality	

Pre-requisite baseline skills

Linguistic	Social	Organisational	Subject specific
Numerical	Thinking	Other	

See Notes

WSPSEN
Activity Pack

Activity Four: Room Management Plan

Room Management
(Adapted from Thomas (1992) p.89/90 with additions by Cowne (1996))

This exercise assumes that two or more adults work together in a classroom on a regular basis. It is designed to help establish the roles these adults will take in managing the whole class and the needs of individual children with a range of difficulties or disabilities.

Role 1: Activity Manager
Before the lesson
- organises a variety of differentiated tasks and activities with relevant materials and equipment.
- informs individual tutor of goals to be acheived within this lesson.

During the lesson
- ensures each group has relevant resources
- prompts children to start task
- supervises sharing of ideas and resources
- moves around groups giving praise and reward to group members who are busy
- gives minimum attention (preferably only by look or gesture) to those not busy

At the end of the lesson
- pulls the lesson together and shares or celebrates outcomes
- evaluates with individual helper

Role 2: The Individual Helper
Before the lesson
- After discussion with class/subject teacher.
- has a list of pupils requiring help and access to these pupils' individual targets and suggested strategies from IEPs
- prepares relevant sets of resources to work towards these goals

During the lesson
- works through the list of pupils using their prepared pack (about 15 minutes per pupil) using maximum praise and gentle encouragement - aiming at autonomy and self motivation from the pupil.

At the end of the lesson
- helps record individual progress as required

Role 3 (optional)
Role 3 could be to keep certain activities going and cut down interuptions to the individual tutor or the activity manager. This role is most suited to classes with younger children or those where self-help skills of pupils need support.

Planning the lesson: allocating roles to tasks

Some lessons can benefit from more adult help than others. It will help to timetable maximum support to such lessons and not to give blanket support on time tables regardless of lesson structures. This may require very flexible use of support. Extra support is most valuable when children are working in groups or in mixtures of tasks requiring sharing of ideas or materials. Skillful support from an adult can enhance group work but most not dominate it. The adult may be able to mediate learning by questioning prompting but also by knowing when to stand back and let the pupils make decisions.

Some tasks need high adult intervention, others medium to low intervention. The roles of **Activity Manager (AM)** and **Individual Tutor (IT)** will change according to types of tasks. In some lession both AM and IT can move amongst groups, stopping to stimulate discussion or more children on problem solving activities. In other lessons, the IT will be allocated to only one or two group tasks.

Lesson Planning using support

Instructions

Plan a lesson of approximately an hour's length for an age group you are familiar with. You will have two adults in the room all the time. A third may be available on occasions. Decide on a topic you know is demanding to teach to this group without support.

Plan group work and adult roles of **AM, IT** and other, and type of task (high, medium, low adult intervention). Use boxes in grid to note main tasks and what each will need to support. Prepare materials. Remember pupils need to know how to work in classrooms where adult have different roles. They need to know that these roles may change from day to day. Establish pupil knowledge of how the adults are working to support learning. Pupils must value both adult roles and understand classroom rules about intervening or asking for help.

WSPSEN - Activity Pack
Activity Four

Room Management Plan

The class has 5 group activities. Pupils may change from their first task to a second or third task during time of lesson. Describe each task. Groups may be mixed ability. Two adults work together in this lesson or a regular basis. A third is sometimes available. Plan what the adults roles will be within this lesson for each of the tasks.

	Group 1 Task	Group 2 Task	Group 3 Task	Group 4 Task	Group 5 Task
Description of task resources and intended learning outcomes					
Role of Activity Manager					
Role Individual Helper					
Other role if available State role and preparation needed					

WSPSEN - Activity Pack
Activity Four

Room Management Plan

<u>Worked example</u> - Pupil groups will change activities and move to next task within planned time.

	Group 1 Task	Group 2 Task	Group 3 Task	Group 4 Task	Group 5 Task
Description of tasks and resources and intended learning outcomes	Planning a story board	Planning a story board	Drafting the story	Correcting work and illustrating their story sequence	Looking at books to choose a story to tell. Reading these to a partner
	Sequencing; beginning, middle and end. Learning to plan in advance of writing	Using pictures to see sequence, a known story writing a sentence with each	Writing story from yesterdays plan - may need words	Reading their own work and deciding on suitable pictures	Understanding story sequence. Looking at Beginnings, Middles & Ends.
Role of Activity Manager	Moves round on task. See AM description	Supports this group to stay on task, gives help with finding words (for spelling) →	Gives help with where to look for words (for spelling) →	Moves round →	Moves round
Role of Individual Helper	Supports group by explaining task and encouraging ideas (15 mins)		Helps target pupils with this (15 mins)		Helps target pupils with this task (15 - 20 minutes into the lesson)

WSPSEN
Activity Pack

Activity Five:
Information Flows for IEP writing and reviewing in large schools

Step 1. Define any problems with existing ways of writing and reviewing IEPs for pupils on Stages 2-5 of the SEN register. Check:
- Does everyone understood what an IEP is and what it must achieve?

Step 2. Brainstorm solutions for identified problems - prioritise outcomes.

Step 3. List existing record-keeping systems, parents' meetings etc.
- How can the SEN work fit in with these existing systems?

Step 4. Decide who could be expected to write IEPs for each of the Stages 2, 3, 4 and 5 of the Code of Practice.
- Remember; it is unlikely that the SENCO can do it all. Which should they be involved in and how will this work? Stages 3 and 4 *must* involve the SENCO.

Step 5. Decide who has information the plan writer will need.
- How will this be collected?

Step 6. Decide who will need information from the IEP when written.
- In what manner will it be sent round to colleagues?

Step 7. Draw up your schools' Information Flow System (see model diagram).

Step 8. Checks:
- Have pupil views been included?
- Do pupils understand their own targets?
- How will parents be kept informed and be part of the review process?
- How will action or plans be taken into classrooms, supported and monitored?
- What resource implications are here?
- Who will need to be informed of the Information Flow System and its implications?
- How will the review cycle work?
- Do we need any new forms to help the process? Who will design these?

Step 9. Form into a policy or guideline and inform staff.

Step 10. How will this be evaluated? Set a time scale and methods for evaluation.
- How long will this be on trial before evaluation?
- Whose views will be requested for evaluation?
- What success criteria could there be?

WSPSEN
Activity Pack

Activity Five:
Information Flows for IEP writing and reviewing in large schools

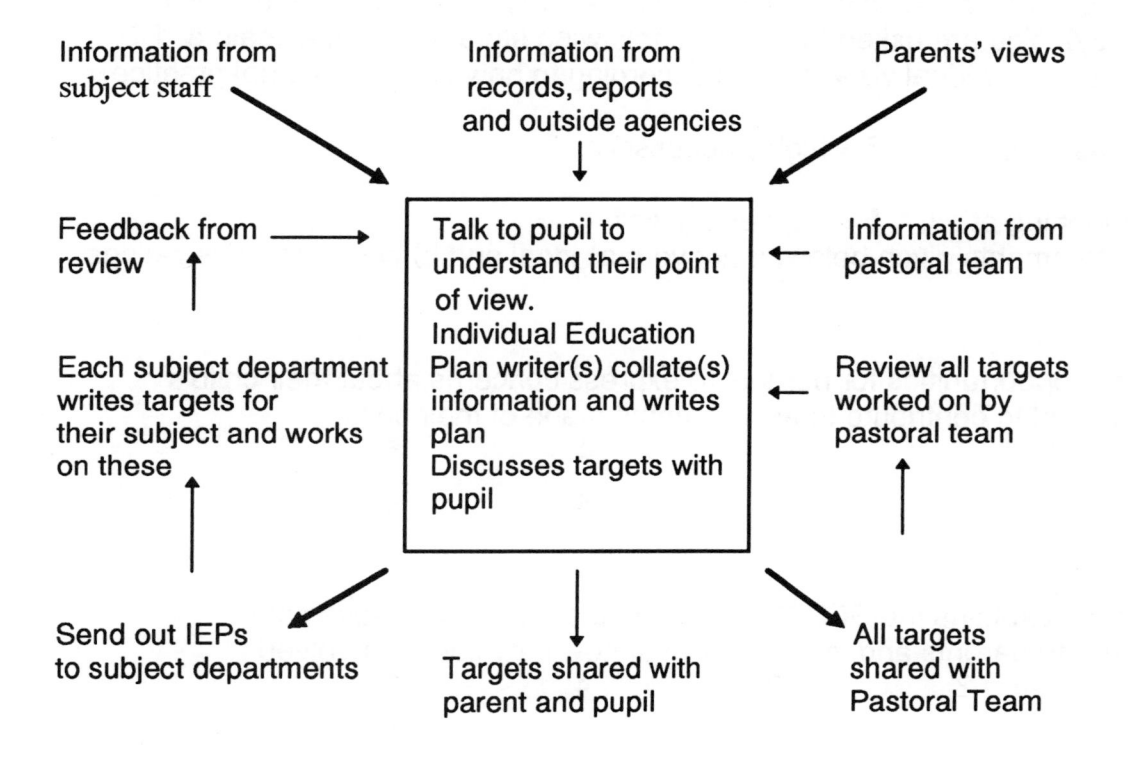

Information from subject staff →

Information from records, reports and outside agencies ↓

Parents' views ↘

Feedback from review → ↑

**Talk to pupil to understand their point of view.
Individual Education Plan writer(s) collate(s) information and writes plan
Discusses targets with pupil**

← Information from pastoral team

← Review all targets worked on by pastoral team ↑

Each subject department writes targets for their subject and works on these ↑

↙ Send out IEPs to subject departments

↓ Targets shared with parent and pupil

↘ All targets shared with Pastoral Team

This diagram is a model to show information flow to and from the IEP Plan writer. Use it in conjunction with Activity 5 to design a system for your own school.

WSPSEN
Activity Pack

Activity Six: Review for Parents Policy

Reviewing your Policy for Parents as an aspect of your whole SEN policy.
This exercise is organised in the same way as Activity 2 (Reviewing the Whole School Policy). You are asked to mark the following statements on a scale of 1-5 a) according to your ideal view, and, b) according to how you view actual practice.
For line a:
1 = not necessary,   5 = highly necessary
For line b:
1 = not happening at all,   5 = happening well
Using the statements given below, mark your a) ideal and b) actual practice ratings.

1. There are opportunities for parents to express concerns about their child's progress and to contribute to assessments made of their child.
    a) 1   2   3   4   5
    b) 1   2   3   4   5

2. The school explains the SEN Register and the 5 staged assessment procedure to parents and informs them of how they can be involved.
    a) 1   2   3   4   5
    b) 1   2   3   4   5

3. Parents are involved in review meetings of individual education plans and are encourage to help the decisions making processes in choosing targets and strategies to implement these.
    a) 1   2   3   4   5
    b) 1   2   3   4   5

4. Parents are involved in the annual review process for pupils with statements and work in partnership with others to choose targets for the next year.
    a) 1   2   3   4   5
    b) 1   2   3   4   5

5. There are clearly defined complaints procedures in respect of provision for SENCO which are known to parents.
    a) 1   2   3   4   5
    b) 1   2   3   4   5

6. The School informs parents of support available within the school and services provided in the LEA for children with SEN and how these can be accessed.
   a) 1   2   3   4   5
   b) 1   2   3   4   5

7. The school SEN policy is available to parents on a readable, accessible format.
   a) 1   2   3   4   5
   b) 1   2   3   4   5

8. Parents are offered opportunities to express their views about SEN policy and provision and its development with school.
   a) 1   2   3   4   5
   b) 1   2   3   4   5

9. Parents are offered contact with local or national voluntary organisations which provide information, advice or counselling.
   a) 1   2   3   4   5
   b) 1   2   3   4   5

10. All information is given in community languages or is accessible in other ways to parents with communication difficulties.
    a) 1   2   3   4   5
    b) 1   2   3   4   5

11. Meetings are conducted in a manner which helps parents to feel confident and be able to make positive contributions.
    a) 1   2   3   4   5
    b) 1   2   3   4   5

12. Add a sentence of your own and rank this also.
    a) 1   2   3   4   5
    b) 1   2   3   4   5

Discussion groups can then use this data to identify priority development areas.

Source Lists

Source List 1: Assessment tools and tests: resources
(unless otherwise stated all material is published by NFER/NELSON: Windsor)

Early years

Bury Infant Checklist. (1980) Pearson, L. & Quinn, J. A development checklist for 5 year olds.
Concepts of Print Test. (1979) Clay, M. Beginning readers. Heinemann Publishers.
Early Years Assessment and Development. Curtis, A. & Wignal, M. 4–6 years – Designed for use in infant schools.
Early Years, easy screen. Clerebugh, J., Hart, K., Rider, K. & Turner, K. 4–5 years.
Larr Test of Emergent Literacy. Downing, J., Schaefer, B. & Ayrs, D. 3–5 years.
Portage Early Education programme. Cameron, S. & White, M. 0-6 years.

Tests of General Ability

British Picture Vocabulary Scale. (1982) Dunn, L., Dunn, L. M., Whelton, C., Pintile, D. 2-18 years.
Ravens Progressive Matrices and Vocabulary Scales. (1956) Raven, J. C. (3 levels available)

Screening Programmes

Quest – Identifying children with reading and writing difficulties. Robertson, A., Henderson, A., Fisher, J. & Gibson, M. 7–8 years.
Stott, D., Green, L. & Francis, J. (1983) *The Guide to the Child's Learning Skills.* NARE Publications.

Reading Tests: Individual

Individual Reading Analysis. (1990) Vincent, D., De la Mare, M. & Arnold, H. 5/6–10 years.
Neale Analysis of reading ability. Neale, M. 5–13 years. Bookbinder, G. (1976)
Salford Sentence Reading Test. 6–10.6 years. Hodder and Stoughton.

Group Reading Tests

Edinburgh Reading Test. Stages 7–9.0 yrs, 8.6–10.6 yrs, 10–12.6yrs 12–16.0 yrs.
NFER/NELSON Reading Tests. Sets 6–13.3, 8.3–15.3

Material for Miscue Analysis

Arnold, H. (1995) *Diagnostic Reading Record.* Hodder and Stoughton.

Specialist Programmes

Locke, A. *Living Language.* A flexible programme for teaching language to group and individuals.

Spelling

Vernon, P.E. (1977). *Graded word spelling test.* Hodder and Stoughton.
Daniels, J. C. and Diack, H. (1958) *Standard Reading Tests.* Hart Davis Education.
Peters, M. L. (1985) *Spelling Caught or Taught: A New Look.* Cambridge Institute.
Hornsby, B. & Shear (1974) *Resource for Spelling.* Heinemann
Brand, V. (1987) *Spelling made easy: Multi-sensory structured spelling.* Baldock: Egon Ltd.

Source List 2: Further reading

Information about disabilities

Chapman, E. K. & Stone, J. M. (1988) *The Visually Handicapped Child in your classroom.* London: Cassell.
Sugden, D. & Wright, H. C. (1995) *Helping your child with movement difficulties.* University of Leeds: School of Education.
Tingle, M. (1990) *The Motor Impaired Child.* Windsor: NFER/Nelson.
Webster, A. & McConnell, C. (1987) *Children with Speech and Language Difficulties.* London: Cassell.
Webster, A. & Wood, D. (1989) *Children with Hearing Impairments.* London: Cassell.

Information for designing individual programmes

Branwhite, T. (1986) *Designing Special Programmes – A Handbook for teachers of children with learning difficulties.* London: Methuen.
Bryant, P. & Bradley, L. (1985) *Children's Reading Problems.* Oxford: Blackwell.
Cooper, P. et al (1995) *Helping them to learn – Curriculum enrichment for children with emotional and behavioural difficulties.* Stafford: NASEN Publications.
Merrett, F. & Wheldall, K. (1990) *Positive teaching in the primary school.* Paul Chapman.
Moss, G. (ed) (1995) *The Basics of Special Needs.* London: Routledge. A survival pack for the classroom teacher.
Mudd, L. (1994) *Effective Spelling – A practical guide for teachers.* Bury St. Edmunds: Hodder and Stoughton.
Sassoon, R. (1990) *Handwriting: a new perspective.* Cheltenham: Stanley Thornes Ltd.
Walker, R. & Adelman, C. (1975) *A Guide to Classroom Observation.* London: Methuen.
Westmacott, E. V. S. (1981) *Behaviour can change.* Macmillan Education.
Wolfendale, S. (ed) (1993) *Assessing Special Educational Needs.* London: Cassell.

Differentiation

George, D. (1992) *The Challenge of the Able Child.* London: Fulton.
Novak, J. D. & Gowin, D. B. (1984) *Learning how to learn.* Cambridge: University Press.
Reid, D. J. & Hodson, D. (1987) *Science for All.* London: Cassell Educational.
Spillman, J. (1991) 'Decoding Differentiation'. *Special Children*, January 1991.
Stradling, R. Saunders, L. & Weston, P. (1991) *Differentiation in Action.* London: DES/HMSO.
Wallace, B. (1983) *Teaching the very able child.* London: Ward Lock Educational.
Wiltshire County Council, Trowbridge (1993) *Differentiating the Secondary Curriculum.*
Entitlement for all. A series on each National Curriculum Subject, London: Fulton.

Policy Making

Council for Disabled Children (1995) *Schools' SEN Policy Pack*, London National Children's Bureau.
Dean, J. (1996) *Managing Special Needs in the Primary School.* London: Routledge.
Gordon, M. & Smith, H. (1995) *Special Educational Needs – A Secondary School Approach.* NASEN Publications.
Hornby, G., Davis, G., Taylor, G. (1995) *The Special Educational Needs Co-ordinators Handbook: A guide for implementing the Code of Practice.* London: Routledge.
Luton, K. (1995) *Development for Special Educational Needs – A primary school approach.* NASEN Publishers.
Luton, K., Booth, G., Leadbetter, J., Tee, G. & Wallace, F. (1991) *Positive Strategies for behaviour management: A whole school approach to discipline.* Windsor: NFER/NELSON.
A pack of materials offering support in developing a whole-school approach to managing behaviour, as recommended by the Elton report (1989) on discipline in schools,
Moseley, J. (1993) *Turn your school around.* LDA.
Moss, G. (1994/95) 'The Role of the SENCO', No 78 Oct 94
    The Code of Practice Stage 3, No 81 Feb 95
    'Managing teaching and non-teaching staff', No 84 May 95
    'Policy and Review', No 85 July 95
    'Quality for All, Staff Development', No 87 Sept 95
(in *Special Children* series on managing SEN, Nos 78–87)
Pearson, L. & Lindsay, G. (1986) *Special Needs in the Primary School: Identification and Intervention.* Windsor: NFER/Nelson.
Ramasut, A. (ed) (1989) *Whole School Approaches to Special Needs.* The Falmer Press.
Thomas, G. & Feiler, A. (1988) *Planning for special needs – A whole-school approach* Oxford: Blackwell.
Topping, K. & Wolfendale, S. (1985) *Parental Involvement in Children's Reading.* Beckenham: Croom Helm.
Wolfendale, S. (1987) *Primary Schools and Special Needs: Policy, Planning and Provision.* London: Cassell Educational.

Special needs assistants training materials

Balshaw, M. H. (1991) *Help in the Classroom*. London: Fulton.
Clayton, T. (1992) 'support for special needs', *Support for Learning*, Vol. 7, No 4.
Fox, G. (1993) *A Handbook for Special Needs Assistants*. London: Fulton.
Working together. The OPTIS Guide for non-teaching staff working with pupils with SEN. Oxford: OPTIS.
Core Material, Responding to Individual Needs; Supporting Learning Difficulties; Physical & Sensory Difficulties Emotional & Behavioural Difficulties; Communication Difficulties.
Accredited training for support assistants is being organised in many LEAs.
Courses are accredited by:
City & Guilds
The Open University
And various colleges using NVQ competencies courses. For further information ask you local Further Education College or your SEN Inspector.
Access through Careers Centres, TAP (Training Access Points) Your local TEC (Training and Enterprise Council)

Source List 3: List of Voluntary Organisations

General

Advisory Centre for Education (ACE) Ltd
Unit 1B, Aberdeen Studios
22 Highbury Grove, London
N5 2EA
Tel: 0171 354 8318 (Business)
Tel: 0171 354 8321 (Advice)

CSIE – Centre for Studies on Integration in Education
415 Edgware Road, London
NW2 6NB
Tel: 0181 452 8642

Contact a family
170 Tottenham Court Road, London
W1P OHA
Tel: 0171 383 3555

Council for Disabled Children
C/O National Children's Bureau
8 Wakley Street, London
EC1V 7QE
Tel: 0171 278 9441

Disability Equality in Education
78 Mildmay Grove, London
N1 4PJ

Disabled Living Foundation
380–384 Harrow Road, London
W9 2HU
Tel: 0171 289 6111

Independent Panel for Special Education Advice
22 Warren Hill Road
Woodbridge, Suffolk
IP12 4DU

Integration Alliance – In Touch
10 Norman Road
Sale, Cheshire
M33 3DF
Tel: 0161 962 4441

Kids
80 Wayneflete Square, London
W10 6UD
Tel: 0181 969 2817

NASEN
Membership Department and Publications
NASEN House
4/5 Amber Business Village
Amber Close
Amington, Tamworth
Staffs, B77 4RP

National Toy Libraries Association
66 Churchway, London
NW1 1LT
Tel: 0171 387 9592

Network 81
1–7 Woodfield Terrace
Chapel Hill, Stansted, Essex
CM24 8AJ
Tel: 01279 647415

Parents in Partnership
Unit 2, Ground Floor
70 South Lambeth Road, London
SW8 1RL
Tel: 0171 735 7733

Rathbone Society
1st Floor, The Excalibur Building
77 Whitworth Street, Manchester
M1 6EZ

Specific

AFASIC (overcoming speech impairments)
347 Central Market, Smithfield, London, EC1A 9NH

British Dyslexia Association
98 London Road, Reading, Berkshire, RG1 5AU

British Epilepsy Association
Anstey House, 40 Hanover Square, Leeds, LS1 BE

Cystic Fibrosis Research Trust
Alexandra House, 5 Blyth Road, Bromley, Kent, BR1 3RS

Downs Syndrome Association
153–5 Mitcham Road, London, SW17 9PG

Foundation for Conductive Education
6th Floor, Clathorpe House, 30 Hagley Road,
Edgbaston, Birmingham, B16 8QY

Invalid Children's Aid – Nationwide ICAN
Barbican City Gate, 1–3 Dufferin Street, London, EC1Y 8NA

MENCAP
123 Golden Lane, London, EC1Y 0RT

MIND
Granta House, 15–19 Broadway, London, E15 4BQ

National Autistic Society
276 Willesden Lane, London, NW2 5RB

Royal National Institute for the Blind
224 Great Portland Street, London, W1N 6AA

Royal National Institute for the Deaf
105 Gower Street, London, WC1E 6AH

SCOPE (formally Spastics Society)
16 Fitzroy Square, London, W1P 5HQ

SENSE
11–13 Clifton Terrace, Finsbury Park, London, N43 SR

SKILL
(National Bureau for Handicapped Students)
336 Brixton Road, London, SW9 7AA

Appendices

Appendix 1

Categories of disability used by LEAs from 1959
These were listed as:

a) blind pupils – pupils whose sight is so defective they require education by methods not using sight.
b) partially sighted pupils – educated by special methods involving use of sight.
c) deaf pupils.
d) partially hearing pupils.
e) educationally subnormal pupils.
f) epileptic pupils – pupils who by reason of epilepsy cannot be educated under normal regime.
g) maladjusted pupils – emotional instability or disturbance.
h) physically handicapped pupils.
i) pupils suffering from speech defect.
j) delicate pupils – pupils not falling under any other category who need a change of environment and who cannot without risk to health or educational development be educated under a normal regime of an ordinary school.

Handicapped Pupils and Special Schools Regulation 1959.
The largest category of children requiring special education was those described as educationally subnormal (ESN). These were children who were backward in basic subjects as well as those who were seen as 'dull'. Pupils with severe learning difficulties were not educated in schools at this time.

Appendix 2a
Governors' Responsibilities

The governing body must:

- do their best to secure that the necessary provision is made for any pupil who has SEN.
- secure that, where the 'responsible person' – the head teacher or the appropriate governor – has been informed by the LEA that a pupil has SEN, those needs are known to all who are likely to teach him or her.
- secure that teachers in the school are aware of the importance of identifying, and providing for, those pupils who have SEN.
- consult the LEA; as appropriate, the Funding Authority; and the governing bodies of other schools, when it seems to them necessary or desirable in the interests of co-ordinated special educational provision in the area as a whole.
- report annually to parents on the school's policy for pupils with SEN.
- ensure that the pupil joins in the activities of the school together with pupils who do not have SEN, so far as that is reasonably practical and compatible with the pupil receiving the necessary special educational provision, the efficient education of other children in the school and the efficient use of resources.
- have regard to the Code of Practice when carrying out their duties towards pupils with SEN.

Code of Practice, Par 2.6

Appendix 2b Schedule I Regulation 2(1)

Basic information about the school's special educational provision

1. The objectives of the governing body in making provision for pupils with special educational needs, and of how the governing body's special educational needs policy will contribute towards meeting those objectives.
2. The name of the person who is responsible for co-ordinating the day-to-day provision of education for pupils with special educational needs at the school (whether or not the person is known as the SEN Co-ordinator).
3. The arrangements which have been made for co-ordinating the provision of education for pupils with special educational needs at the school.
4. The admission arrangements for pupils with special educational needs who do not have a statement in so far as they differ from the arrangements for other pupils.
5. The kinds of provision for special educational needs in which the school specialises and any special units.
6. Facilities for pupils with special educational needs at the school including facilities which increase or assist access to the school by pupils who are disabled.

Information about the school's policies for the identification, assessment and provision for all pupils with special educational needs.

7. How resources are allocated to and amongst pupils with special educational needs.
8. How pupils with special educational needs are identified and their needs determined and reviewed.
9. Arrangements for providing access by pupils with special educational needs to a balanced and broadly based curriculum (including the National Curriculum).
10. How pupils with special educational needs engage in the activities of the school together with pupils who do not have special educational needs.
11. How the governing body evaluate the success of the education which is provided at the school to pupils with special educational needs.
12. Any arrangements made by the governing body relating to the treatment of complaints from parents of pupils with special educational needs concerning the provision made at the school.

Information about the school's staffing policies and partnership with bodies beyond the school

13. Any arrangements made by the governing body relating to in-service training for staff in relation to special educational needs.
14. The use made of teachers and facilities from outside the school including links with support services for special educational needs.
15. The role played by the parents of pupils with special educational needs.
16. Any links with other schools, including special schools and the provision made for the transition of pupils with special educational needs between schools or between the school and the next stage of life or education.
17. Links with child health services, social services and educational welfare services and any voluntary organisations which work on behalf of children

Appendix 3a   *Guidance notes on Code of Practice forms*

Record of Concern

This form has proved popular with teachers to collate information about the pupil at Stage 1. Information gathered should include:

- Health records
- Parents' views
- Previous school records
- Professional assessments and letters
- Observations
- Child's viewpoint

The needs of the pupil at this stage will be met by differentiation of normal classroom work. This will be informed by information summarised on the record of concern. Action taken, other information to be sought and special arrangements made can be noted. All this should be reviewed regularly. The majority of pupils will remain at this stage of the Code of Practice assessment.

The Individual Education Plan Form

Once information is collated from the Record of Concern and reviewed it may be dear that some pupils need a more detailed individual education plan. Targets will be set which produce a working document which will inform class teacher's planning: These will be

- Cross-curricular and related to the areas of concern.
- Expressed in precise terms which can be assessed and evaluated.
- Agreed with the pupil.

Step 1 – Collect information about the child from all previous records, interviews with parents, health checks etc. This should have been done at Stage 1 of the Code of Practice stages. Decide on the major areas of concerns and record these. Write down the child's strengths and present known levels of attainment. Discuss the learning difficulties or problem area with the pupil as well as finding out what they feel they can do well. Note any special pastoral and medical arrangements.

Step 2 – Decide on targets for the present plan. These should be as cross-curricular as necessary, but as precisely expressed. They should be written as clear observable behaviours, if not, it will be difficult to measure success in reaching the target. Avoid fuzzies like 'Sean needs to learn to write'. Express this as 'Sean will write three sentences unaided with no more than 3 errors.'

Step 3 – Decide teaching strategies to achieve the targets; include frequency and type of support to be given and any specialist resources needed, or particular contexts required.

Step 4 – Decide on success criteria for each target and how it will be assessed. Link to National Curriculum assessment where possible.

Step 5 – **Important** – Set review date and when it comes round, review the success or otherwise in reaching the targets. Parents' and pupils' views should be recorded.

Step 6 – Set new targets or repeat those already used. Modify support levels, change teaching strategies or success criteria as necessary to set achievable targets.

Step 7 – Teach to new targets.

This process applies at Stages 2-5 of the Code of Practice and should include those with statements. **An IEP is a process over time**. Show as much precise information as possible about what the child can do and what support level is needed to achieve success. Parents should be asked to the review and their views recorded on the form or in other ways as the school policy dictates.

Record of Concern at Stage 1

Child's name   Date of plan   Plan number

_____   _____   _____

DoB:	Age:	NC Year:	Class:

Concerns (Check health records; ask parents' views)

Present levels of attainment/development – pupil's strengths

Action

Review date

Outcome of review

Sheet number:

_____   _____

Individual Education Plan
Child's name

Date of plan   Plan number

Pupil views	Parent's views
Pupil's strengths and attainments	Areas of concern

Learning targets *state these precisely*	Teaching strategies; frequency of support	How progress will be assessed and monitored

Review outcomes

Teacher's name   Date of Review or Annual Review (stage 5)

TARGETS

should be………………………SMART

Specific

Measurable

Attainable

Realistic

Time-bound

TARGETS

Appendix 3b

The relationship between bilingual learners' language stages and the Code of Practice stages

Bilingual learners are often classified by E2L teachers by their stages of development in learning English. This should not be confused with the Code of Practice Stages.

Bilingual Stages

Stage 1 – new to English.
Stage 2 – learning familiarity with English.
Stage 3 – becoming confident in use of English.
Stage 4 – on the way to fluent use of English in most social learning contexts.

Pupils at bilingual Stage 1 should not be put on SEN Register unless they have clearly identified disabilities such as a hearing problem. Pupils at bilingual Stage 1 will often be supported by teachers from a bilingual service (E2L). It takes up to 2 years to develop basic inter-personal communication. E2L teachers can give advice on how to support and teach these pupils to acquire their new language while retaining the use of their own first language.

Things to do

- Find out how long the pupil has been learning English.
- Talk to parents about the child in the home context and what language(s) are spoken at home.
- Check health records and previous educational history.

Read *Assessing the Needs of Bilingual Pupils* Deryn Hall (1995) London: Fulton.

Appendix 4a *Instrumental Enrichment, cognitive functions as expressed by students*

1. INPUT – Gathering all the information we need

- Using senses to gather, clear and complete information.
- Using a plan so we don't miss anything.
- Giving all of this a name so we can talk about it.
- Describing things in terms of where and when they occur.
- Deciding on characteristics which stay the same.
- Organising the information we gather by considering more than one thing at a time.
- Being precise and accurate when it matters.

2. ELABORATION – Using the information we have gathered

- Defining a problem, what we must do and what we must figure out.
- Using only that part of the information that is relevant.
- Having a picture in our mind of what we are looking for and what we aim to do.
- Making a plan which will involve steps needed to reach our goal.
- Remembering various pieces of information we will need.
- Looking for relationships.
- Comparing objects or experiences.
- Finding categories or sets.
- Thinking about 'what if' questions.
- Using logic to defend our opinions.

3. OUTPUT – Expressing the solution to a problem

- Being clear and precise so you can be understood.
- Think things through before you answer and wait before you say something you may regret.
- Don't panic if you can't immediately answer a question, return to it later.
- Carry a picture in your mind for comparison without losing or changing details.

Adapted from Adey and Shayer (1994)

Feuerstein *et al* (1979) lists the nature and focus of cognitive impairments related to his 3 phases of information processing: Input, Elaboration and Output. These include lack of planning, impulsive behaviour, impaired receptive verbal tools, impaired spatial orientation or temporal concepts, inability to define a problem or pursue logical evidence. It is his programme of instrumental enrichment which is designed to overcome these impaired processes and blocked learning.

Appendix 4b   *Summary of Bloom's Taxonomy (adapted from Bloom, B.S., 1965)*

Level 1: Acquiring knowledge
The learner is given information, specific terminology or symbols; the learner masters specific techniques or skills. Acquiring knowledge involves memory, repetition and description. Knowing where and how to find out information is one of the important requisites of knowledge acquisition. Very able pupils need far less time to absorb knowledge and less rehearsal to reach mastery level in skills. Pupils with learning difficulties will need more guidance in making connections, more rehearsal and practice.

Level 2: Comprehension
The learner is required to demonstrate that knowledge has been acquired by:
Translation – Explaining meanings and selecting information to answer questions.
Interpretation – Interpreting and reordering facts contrasting or classifying these according to specific criteria.
Extrapolation – Determining consequences and implications.
   The first of these ways, translation, is the most commonly used by teachers. Predicting outcomes and discussing implications may require working at a higher level of thinking.

Level 3: Application
The learner is required to:
- Use knowledge to solve problems.
- Translate methods and techniques to new solutions.
- Bring general principles to bear in new questions.

Level 4: Analysis
The learner is involved in breaking down the whole to clarify the relationships between constituent parts. This involves:
- Differentiating fact from fiction.
- Identifying hidden meanings.
- Finding themes and patterns.
- Understanding systems and organisations.

Level 5: Synthesis
The learner is required to create new relationships, combine elements to form a new whole. This involves:
- Organising sets of ideas to make new statements.
- Developing plans to test a hypothesis.
- Creating a new form of classifying data.
- Discovering new relationships.
- Inventing, changing and improving ideas.
- Thinking creatively and risk making new connections.

Level 6: Evaluation
The learner goes through a process of appraising, assessing and criticising which involves:
- Judging on the basis of logical evidence.
- Verifying the worth of evidence or proof.
- Evaluation according to specified criteria.
- Comparing contrasting theories or generalisations.
- Arbitrating in controversial arguments.

This requires personal decision making based on reasoned and logical argument, supported by evidence.

Appendix 8a *Statement of Special Educational Needs: Appendices*

(Statutory Instruments p.30 Code of Practice, end section)

Appendices A, B and C offer parents different ways of contributing; Appendix A allows parents to make representations if they wish to do so. Appendix B allows evidence e.g. private professional reports requested by parents. Appendix C, the parents' own advice about their child. In most cases Appendix C is completed but it is possible for the LEA to issue a statement without any of these three, if the parent does not wish to reply to the request.

Appendix D is teacher advice, usually from the school, but specialist teachers' advice is added where applicable or where the child is not in a school.

Appendix E – Medical Advice – (doctors and therapists).

Appendix F – Psychological Advice.

Appendix G – Social Service Advice. This is not completed if the child is not known to social services.

Appendix H – Other advice obtained by the Authority (as needed).

The LEA must request advice within the tight time limits set by the Code of Practice (see Sections 4 & 5).

Appendix 8b *The SEN Management Form*

This is for the SENCO to collate information on to one form for easy reference. Once opened it can be updated as necessary. Only one form is needed per pupil. This cuts down unnecessary copying of information onto the frequently changing classroom IEP form. The form should record:

- National Curriculum year group.
- Schools attended.
- Outside services and agencies involved with dates of reports or advice given.
- IEP review dates (and only for a few pupils).
- Dates for a Stage 4 assessment request.
- Date of Stage 4 assessment starting.
- Date of draft statement.
- Dates of annual reviews.

Information which will not change over time could also be recorded on this form, for example, the mother tongue spoken by the child, how long English has been spoken and the position in the family. This will vary according to school policy.

SEN Management Form

Child's name Date of Birth Names of those with parental responsibility

_____ _____ _____

NC Year ———————————————————————————————————

Schools attended	LEA

Agency/Support Service involvement	Date of report

Outside Agency and Support Service involvement

Dates	IEP Reviews Notes	Other information and notes

Appendix 9a

Different ways of observing children

Observation is a way of finding out more, but first it is necessary to ask: *Why observe?* Answers could be:

- As a means of generating hypotheses.
- As a means of answering specific questions. How often does a child do that?
- As a way to better understand children and their viewpoints and behaviours.

This last point is the most relevant to those wishing to learn about pupil perspectives.

Next ask: What should we observe?

This could be a matter of choosing the scale of the focus, either:
- Large units of activity, e.g. playground behaviour, or
- Specific activities e.g. reading strategies, or
- Facial expressions, gestures, eye movements within specific contexts.

Next ask: *How should the observations be done?*

This could be in the form of:
- Diaries; biographies over time e.g. day, week.
- Single episode recording.
- Time sampling; e.g. one minute every 15 minutes.
- Event sampling; record specific type of event wherever it happens.
- Tracking; observing child in different contexts or with different adults over a fixed period.

What form will recording take?

- Narrative descriptions.
- Prepared checklists to tick or mark with symbols.
- Audio or video tape analysis.

All have advantages and some suit certain techniques best. Narrative is necessary for diaries, tracking and events sampling. Checklists are best for time sampling. A mixture of methods may produce the best all round picture.

Cautions

- All observations take time – analysis can be even more time consuming.
- Focus as much as possible; be selective but be aware of bias from this selection.
- Note what you see; not your inferences, draw no conclusions without evidence.
- Be aware of observer bias – two observers may produce a clearer picture of reality.
- Try to see things from the pupils' perspective, not yours.
- Prepare carefully to avoid missing things because you can't record quickly or accurately enough.
- Warn colleagues of your activities and don't underestimate pupils. They might ask 'what are you doing?' if your behaviour is too peculiar!
- What part will spoken language play? will this be recorded with the observation and if so, how?
- How valid are your observations? can you check these with the child?

Examples

Time Sampling
- Useful when behaviours to be observed are frequent.
- Or, when behaviours are distinct and early recognised.

Advantages
- It takes less time if prepared well.
- Provides quantifiable data.
- Useful for baseline information.

Disadvantages
- Doesn't tell much about pupil perspectives.
- Omits context and interaction between behaviours.
- Can distort reality because cause and effect may not be noted.

Event Sampling
- Useful to learn more about a selective type of behaviour in detail.
- Or when a whole event can be recorded and analysed.
- Where context – antecedents and consequences can be noted – good for the ABC analysis of behaviour.
- Can be used for infrequent events.
- Pupil views can be included.

Disadvantages
- More difficult to prepare for thoroughly.
- Needs more analysis after the observation.

Tracking
- Useful to find out the effect of different teachers, experiences on a child to find out reasons for a problem.

Disadvantages
- Taking the time to do this may be difficult.
- Colleagues need to agree and understand purposes.
- Being inconspicuous may be difficult. The observer may make the pupil behave differently.
- Focus on one pupil might be difficult to disguise and could cause embarrassment. Observer's activity must be plausible to the peer group.

The best way may be to use a mixture of techniques and data and to balance one with another.

Remember observation material is confidential and must be used to provide information to solve a problem or gain useful information to **help the child or children.** Once used it should not be kept in any way that could identify the pupil. Pupils and parents have rights. Ask permission if at all possible in principle, even if not explaining all the techniques. Observation will provide data, set up hypotheses and is one source of information, but pupils' views will need to be collected as well as the views of parents and other professionals to check out its validity.

Appendix 9b

Example of questionnaire for primary pupils

Use the faces to find out how children feel about your area of enquiry. Ask your questions orally and use the first two to get the group used to the idea of colouring in or ticking the face that is most like 'how they feel when ...' for example, watching your favourite TV programme. Then ask about how they feel when ... asking the research questions. (Used by the ILEA Research for 8 year olds looking into pupils' views about learning to read and write from ILEA Research and Statistics 1988).

	😀	🙂	😐	🙁	☹️
1.					
2.					
3.					
4.					

Appendix 9c

Definition of Parent from Glossary of Code and Children Act
A parent includes any person:

- Who is not a natural parent of the child but who has parental responsibility for him or her, or
- Who has care of the child.

Parental responsibility under section 2 of the Children Act falls upon:

- All mothers and fathers who were married to each other at the time of the child's birth.
- Mothers who were not married to the father at the time of the child's birth.
- Fathers who were not married to the mother at the time of the child's birth, but who have parental responsibility either by agreement with the child's mother or through a court order.

Bibliography

Adey, P. & Shayer, M. (1994) *Really Raising Standards: Cognitive Intervention and Academic Achievement.* London: Routledge.

Alexander, R., Rose, J. & Woodhead, C. (1992) *Curricula organisation and classroom practice in primary schools.* DES, London: HMSO.

Ainscow, M., Muncey, J. (1981) *SNAP Workshop Guides.* Coventry: LEA.

Ainscow, M. & Tweddle, D. (1988) *Encouraging Classroom Success.* London: Fulton.

Audit Commission (1992a) *Getting in on the Act – Provision for pupils with Special Educational Needs: The National Perspective.* London: HMSO.

Audit Commission/HMI (1 992b) *Getting the Act Together – Provision for Pupils with Special Educational Needs: A Management Handbook for School and Local Education Authorities.* London: HMSO.

Audit Commission/HMI (1994c) *The Act Moves on 1 – Progress in Special Educational Needs.* Audit Commission bulletin, London: HMSO.

Balshaw, M. H. (1991) *Help in the Classroom.* London: Fulton.

Baskind, S. & Thompson, D. (1995) 'Using assistants to support the educational needs of pupils with learning difficulties: The sublime or the ridiculous', *Educational and Child Psychology,* Vol. 12, No 2 pp.46–57.

Bennett, N. (1976) *Teaching Styles and Pupil Progress.* London: Open Books.

Bennett, N. (1984) *The Quality of Pupil Learning Experiences.* London: Lawrence Erbaum Associates.

Bentley, A. (1995) 'Allocation of the school's resources to meet Special Educational Needs', in Discussion papers II, pp 57–64 *Schools' SEN Policy Pack.* London: National Children's Bureau.

Blagg, N., Ballinger, M. & Gardner, R. (1988) *Somerset Thinking Skills.* Basil Blackwell & Somerset County Council.

Bloom, B. A. (1965) *Taxonomy of Educational Objectives.* London: Longman.

Booth, T. (1982) 'National Perspectives' – *Unit 10 Course E241 – Special Needs in Education.* Milton Keynes: Open University.

Bruner, J. (1968) *Towards a Theory of Instruction,* New York: W. W. Norton.

Campbell, K. (1995) 'How schools might work more effectively with social service departments', Discussion Papers V pp.7–11, *Schools' SEN Policy Pack.* London: National Children's Bureau.

Clay, M. (1993) *Reading Recovery.* Auckland: Heineman Education.

Cowne, E. A. & Norwich, B. (1987) *Lessons in Partnership,* Bedford Way Paper, No 31. London: Institute of Education.

Cowne, E. A. (1993) *Conversational uses of the Repertory Grid for Personal Learning and the Management of Change in Special Educational Needs.* Unpublished PHD Thesis. Uxbridge: Brunel University.

Curtis, A. M. (1986) *A Curriculum for the Pre-school Child – Learning to Learn.* Windsor NFER: Nelson.

Dale, N. (1996) *Working with Families with Special Needs: Partnership and Practice.* London: Routledge

Dearing, R. (1994) *The National Curriculum and its Assessment.* London: SCAA.

de Bono, E. (1987) *CoRT Thinking Program.* Chicago: Science Research Associates.

DES (1944) *Education Act.* London: HMSO.

DES (1959) *Handicapped Pupils and Special Educational Needs Regulations.*

DES (1967) *Children and their Primary Schools.* (The Plowden Report) London: HMSO.

DES (1970) *Handicapped Children Act.* London: HMSO.

DES (1978) *Special Educational Needs: Report of the committee of Enquiry into the Education of Handicapped Children and Young People.* (The Warnock Report) London: HMSO.
DES (1980) *Education Act.* London: HMSO.
DES (1981) *Education Act.* London: HMSO.
DES (1983) *Assessment and Statements of Special Educational Needs,* Joint Circular with DHSS & LEA. Circular 1/83. London: HMSO.
DES (1983, 1984, 1985) *The In-service Training Grants Scheme,* Circulars London: HMSO.
DES (1986) *Education Act.* London: HMSO.
DES, Black, P. J. (1987) *Task Group on Assessment and Testing – A Report.*
DES (1988) *Education Reform Act.* London: HMSO.
DES (1990) *Staffing for Children with Special Educational Needs.* Circular 11/90 London: HMSO.
DfE (1993) *The Education Act.* London: HMSO.
DfE (1994a) *The Code of Practice on the Identification and Assessment of Special Educational Needs.* London: HMSO.
DfE (1994b) *Special Educational Needs: A guide for parents.*
DfE (1994c) *The Organisation of Special Education.* Circular 6/94. London: HMSO.
DfE (1994d) *Pupils with problems* (The 6 Pack) Circulars 8/94 -13/94 London: HMSO.
DfE (1 994e) *Special Educational Needs Tribunals: How to appeal.* London: DfE Publications Centre.
DHSS (1989) *The Children Act.* London: HMSO.
Diamond, C. (1993) 'A reconsideration of the role of SEN Support Services – Will they get in on the Act?', *Support for Learning,* Vol. 8, No 3, pp.9 1-98.
Diamond, D. C. (1995) 'How to get the best from your flexible friend – A Review of the working relationship between schools and SEN Support Services', *Support for Learning,* Vol. 10, No 2, pp.63–69.
Donaldson, M. (1978) *Children's Minds.* Glasgow: Fontana.
Dyson, A. (1990) 'Effective Learning Consultancy – A future role for SENCOs', *Support for Learning,* Vol. 5, No 3, pp. 116–127.
Dyson, A. (1991) 'Rethinking roles, rethinking concepts: special needs teachers in mainstream schools.' *Support for Learning,* Vol 6, No2, pp.51–60.
Dyson, A. (1995) 'Thriving on chaos? Co-ordinators, conflict and uncertainty' Discussion Papers II, pp.63–66 *Schools' SEN Pack.* London: National Children's Bureau.
Evans, J., Everard, B., Friend, J., Glaser, A., Norwich, B. & Welton, J. (1981) *Decision making for special educational needs – an inter-service resource pack.* London: University of London, Institute of Education.
Evans, J. & Lunt, I. (1994) *Markets, Competition, Vulnerability, some effects of recent Legislation on pupils with Special Educational Needs.* London: Institute of Education & Tufnell Press (London File series).
Feuerstein, R., Rand,Y., Hoffmann, M. & Millar, M. (1980) *Instrumental Enrichment – An Intervention Programme for Cognitive Modifiability.* Baltimore, M. D: University Park Press.
Fish, J. (1985) *Educational Opportunities for All.* Report of the committee reviewing provision to meet SEN. ILEA. (The Fish Report).
Fish, J. (1989) *What is Special Education?* Milton Keynes: Open University Press.
Fish, J. & Evans, J. (1995) *Managing Special Education Codes, Charters and Competition.* Buckingham: Open University Press.
Fisher, R. (1990) *Teaching children to think.* Hemel Hempstead: Simon & Schuster.
Frederickson, N. (1993) 'Using Soft Systems Methodology to re-think Special Needs' in Dyson A., Gains, C. (eds) – '*Rethinking Special Needs in Mainstream Schools towards the year 2000'* pp.1–21. London: Fulton.
Galloway, D. (1985) *Schools, Pupils and Special Educational Needs.* London: Croom Helm
Galton, M. (1987) 'An Oracle Chronicle – A decade of classroom research' – *Teaching and Teacher Education 3.4* London: Routledge & Kegan Paul.

Galton, M. & Simon (1980) *Progress and Performance in the Primary School.* London: Routledge & Kegan Paul.

Gardner, D. & Sandow, S. (1995) *Advocacy, Self advocacy.* London: Fulton.

Gascoigne, E. (1995) *Working with Parents as Partners in SEN.* London: Fulton.

George, D. (1992) *The Challenge of the Able Child.* London: Fulton.

Gilbert, C. & Hart, M. (1990) *Towards Integration – Special Needs in an Ordinary School.* London: Kogan Page.

Gipps, C. (1992) *What we know about effective primary teaching.* London: Institute of Education & Tufnell Press.

Gipps, C., Gross, H. & Goldstein, H. (1987) *Warnocks Eighteen Per Cent – Children with Special Needs in Primary Schools.* Lewes: Falmer.

Gipps, C. & Stobart, G. (1990) *Assessment – A Teachers Guide to the Issues.* Sevenoaks: Hodder and Stoughton.

Greenhalgh, P. (1994) *Emotional Growth and Learning.* London & New York: Routledge.

Goucher, B., Evans, J., Welton, J. & Wedell, K. (1988) *Policy and Provision for Special Educational Needs – Implementing the 1981 Act.* London: Cassell.

Hall, D. (1995) *Assessing the needs of Bilingual Pupils.* London: Fulton.

Hanko, G. (1995) *Special Needs in Ordinary Classrooms: from Staff Support to Staff Development.* Third Edition. London: Fulton.

Hart, S. (1991) 'The Collaborative Classroom' in *Supporting Schools.* McLaughlin and Rouse. London: Fulton.

Hornby, G., Davis, G., Taylor, G. (1995) *The Special Educational Needs Co-ordinators Handbook: A guide for implementing the Code of Practice.* London: Routledge.

Inhelder, B. & Piaget, J. (1958) *The Growth of Logical Thinking.* London: Routledge & Kegan Paul.

Lipman, M., Sharp, M. & Oscanyan, F. (1980) *Philosophy in the Classroom.* Philadelphia: Temple University Press.

Lorenz, S. (1992) 'Supporting Special Educational Needs Assistants in Mainstream Schools', *Educational and Child Psychology,* pp.25–34.

Lunt, I., Evans, J., Norwich, B. & Wedell, K. (1994) *Working together: inter-school collaboration for special needs.* London: Fulton.

Lunt, I., Evans, J. (1994) *Allocating Resources for Special Educational Needs Provision.* Stafford: NASEN.

Marsh, H. (1995) 'Working with Voluntary Organisations' Discussion Papers V pp.23–29
Schools' SEN Pack. London: National Children's Bureau.

Mallett, R. (1995) 'Parents: SEN Policy and practice' in Discussion Papers IV, pp.7–12 *Schools' SEN Policy Pack.* London: National Children's Bureau.

Merton, London Borough of, (1991) '*LEA Guidelines on drawing up and reviewing a Whole School Policy for Special Educational Needs'.* Inspectorate and Advisory Service: Guidelines 3/91 .

McKinlay, I. (1995) 'Help from the Health Service' in Discussion Papers V, pp.15–20 *Schools' SEN Policy Pack.* London: National Children's Bureau.

Mortimore, P., Mortimore, J. with Thomas, H. (1994) *Managing Associate Staff Innovation in primary and secondary schools.* London: Paul Chapman.

Mortimore, P., Sammon, P. Stoll, L., Lewis, D. & Ecob, R. (1988) *School Matters: The Junior Years.* Wells: Open Books.

National Curriculum Council (1989a) '*Implementing the National Curriculum – Participation by pupils with SEN:* Circular No 5. York: NCC.

National Curriculum Council (1989b) *A Curriculum for All – Special Educational Needs in the National Curriculum.* Vol 2.

NFER (1995) *Small steps of progress in the National Curriculum: Final Report Executive summary.*

Norwich, B. (1990a) *Reappraising Special Education.* London: Cassell.

Norwich, B. (1990b) 'How Entitlement can become a restraint' in Daniels, H., Ware, J. *Special Educational Needs and the National Curriculum*. Kogan Page & Institute of Education, London.

Norwich, B. (1995a) 'Individual Education Plans' in Discussion Papers II, pp.23–30 *Schools' SEN Policy Pack*. London: National Children's Bureau.

Norwich, B. (1995b) 'Clusters: inter-school collaboration for Special Educational Needs' in Discussion Papers IV, pp.25–29 *Schools' SEN Policy Pack*. London: National Children's Bureau.

O'Hanlon, C. (1993) 'Changing the school by reflectively re-defining the role of the special needs co-ordinator' in Dyson, A. & Gains, C. (eds) – *Rethinking Special Needs in Mainstream Schools Towards the Year 2000*, pp.99–109 London: Fulton.

OFSTED Framework (1995) *Framework for the inspection of schools*. London: HMSO.

OFSTED (1995) *Promoting High Achievement for Pupils with SEN*. London: HMSO.

Ramjhun, A. F. (1995) *Implementing the Code of Practice for Children with Special Educational Needs: A Practical Guide*. London: Fulton.

Reason, R. (1990) *Reconciling different approaches to intervention*, In P. D. Pumfrey & C. D. Elliott (eds) *Children's Reading, Spelling and Writing Difficulties*. Lewis: Falmer.

Reason, R. & Boote, R. (1994) *Helping Children with Reading and Spelling: A Special Needs Manual*. London: Routledge.

Rieser, R. (1995) 'Developing a Whole School approach to inclusion: Making the most of the Code of Practice and the 1993 Act: A personal view' Discussion Papers III pp.39–46. *Schools' SEN Policy Pack*. London: NCB.

Robson, B. (1989) *Pre-school provision for Children with Special Needs*. London: Cassell.

Russell, P. (1994) 'The Code of Practice New Partnership for children with Special Educational Needs'. *British Journal of Special Education*, Vol 21–22, pp.48–52.

Russell, P. (1995a) 'Policy and Diversity: addressing values and principles when developing a school policy for children with Special Educational Needs' in Discussion Papers I, pp.15-23 *Schools' SEN Policy Pack*. London: National Children's Bureau.

Russell, P. (1995b) 'The Transition Plan' in Discussion Papers IV, pp.57–65. *Schools' SEN Policy Pack*. London: National Children's Bureau.

School Curriculum and Assessment Authority (1995) *Planning the Curriculum at Key Stage 1 & 2*. London: SCAA.

School Curriculum and Assessment Authority (1995) *Managing the Curriculum at Key Stage 4*. London: SCAA.

School Curriculum and Assessment Authority (1995) *Special Educational Needs and Examinations at 16*. London: SCAA.

Skinner, B. F. (1974) *About Behaviourism*. London: Jonathan Cape.

Sutton, A. (1982) 'The Powers that be'. Unit 8, E241 Course material. Milton Keynes: Open University Press.

Thomas, G. (1992) *Effective Classroom Teamwork*. London: Routledge.

Tizard, B. & Hughes, M. (1994) *Young Children Learning*. Glasgow: Fontana.

Tizard, B., Blatchford, P., Burke, J., Farquare, I. & Plewis, I. (1988) *Young Children at School in the Inner City*. Hove: Lawrence Erbaum Assoc.

Tomlinson, S. (1982) *A Sociology of Special Education*. London: Routledge & Kegan Paul.

Vygotsky, L. S. (1978) *Mind in Society*. Massachusetts: Harvard University Press.

Wedell, K. (1980) 'Early identification and compensatory interaction' in Knights, R. M. & Bakker, D. J. *Treatment of Hyperactive and Learning Disordered Children*. Baltimore: University Park Press.

Wedell, K. (1990) 'The 1988 Act and current principles of Special Educational Needs', in Daniels, H. & Ware, J. *Special Educational Needs and the National Curriculum*. Kogan Page & Institute of Education, London.

Weller, K. & Craft, A. (1983) *Making up our Minds: An exploratory study of Instrumental Enrichment*. Schools Council.

Index

Able pupils 24
Admission arrangements 17
Advocacy 91
Affective intervention 44–45
Annual report to parents 13,16
Assessment arrangements 50
    IEP as assessment 80
    of need 23–26
    tools and tests 26, *Source list 1*
Audit Commission reports 11, 60, 72, 73

Behavioural objectives 40
Behavioural science 39
Behavioural Support Service 65
Bilingual learners 24, *Appendix 3b*
Bloom's Taxonomy 43, *Appendix 4b*

Careers services 75
Children Act 10, 75, 92, *Appendix 9c*
Children in care 67
Child Guidance 67
Circulars
    1/83 10
    3/83 10
    11/90 86
    6/94 13, 16, 17, 23, 65, 66, 94, 95, 97
    9/94 66
    13/94 67
Classroom management 45
   organisation 35, 49
   teams 58
Clusters of schools 65, 72
Code of Practice 11, 13, 15, 16–19, 31, 65, 76, 80, 84, 90–91, 94–95, 128, 135
Cognitive development 41
Cognitive intervention 41–44
Collaborative teaching 57
Complaints 95

Developmental curriculum 37–38
Differentiation 18, 53, *Source list 2* 124
   lesson plan for 39, *Activity Pack 3*
   SENCOs role in 46
Disability categories *Appendix 1*
   movement 99
   further reading *Source list 2* 123
Early years
   assessment 26
   curriculum 47
   transition to school 73–74
Education Acts
   1944 8
   1970 9
   1981 9, 10, 93
   1988 Education Reform 8, 10, 36, 93
   1993 11, 15, 93
   summaries in relation to parents 93
Educational psychologists 9, 48, 65, 70
Education Welfare Officer 66–67

Effective schools 13, 15, 99
Effective support 63, 71–73
Emphatic listening 92
Emotional and behavioural difficulties 60, 69
Entitlement curriculum 10, 36
Evaluation
   of whole–school policy 20–21,100
   of SENCO role 101
Examination arrangements 52

Formal operational thinking 41
Further Education Funding Council 75

Grant Maintained schools 19, 57, 70

Health services 66, 69, 70
Hearing impaired service 65, 67, 70

Identification and intervention 78
Inclusive education 99
Individual Education Plans (IEP) 14, 23, **31–32**, 38, 54, 56, 71, *Source list 2*
   as continuous assessment 80
   forms *Appendix 3a*
   review of 32, 78, 80, *Activity Pack 5*
   within differentiation 38
Information flow for IEPs *Activity Pack 5*
Instrumental enrichment 41–42, *Appendix 4a*
In–service 97
Integration arrangements 17–18, 57, 66
Interactive model of SEN 25, 40

Key Stage 1
   assessment 26
   curriculum 48
Key Stage 2
   assessment 27
   curriculum 49
Key Stage 3
   assessment 29
   continuity curriculum 51
   support 69
Key Stage 4
   assessment 30
   curriculum 52
Key issues for SENCOs 13, 47, 49, 50–53

Learning Support Departments 51, 53
Learning Support Services 65, 67, 70
Local Education Authority (LEA) 8–12, 16, 18, 33, 65, 67, 75, 81–85, 99
Local management of schools (LMS) 8, 10, 72, 99

Miscue analysis 28
Modified curriculum 37
Multi–professional
   assessment 10, 11, 81
   decision making 9
   priorities 10
Named Person 68
NASEN 62
National Curriculum 36, 49, 80
National Curriculum Council (NCC) 36
Non-Teaching Assistants (NTA) 59
   job descriptions 48, 57
   training of 59–60
Nursery curriculum 47

Nursery nurse (NNEB) 48

Observation techniques 90, *Appendix 9a*
OFSTED 53, 78, **85–87**
Organisation of files 79–80
Organisation of IEP reviews 80

Parents
   arrangements for 94
   involvement 8, 9, 14, 49, 92
   multi–professional assessment 71
   policy review – *Appendix Pack 6*
   responsibilities – *Appendix 9c*
   rights 14, 92
Partnership with parents 91
Peer–parent reading 48
Philosophy for children 43
Phonological reading approach 48
Policy evaluation 21
   making 24
   review cycle 20–21, *Activity Pack 2*
Portage 47
Post-Dearing revision 36, 52
Psycholinguistic reading approach 48
Pupil
   rights 14
   perspectives 89–90
   problem solving 92
   questionnaires 90, 140
Reading for information 49

Reading recovery 48
Record of Concern form – *Appendix 3a*
Regulation 2(1) – *Appendix 2b*
Regulation 5 p13, 21, *Appendix 2b*
Regulation 15(5) 83
Responsible person 15
Roles and Responsibilities 12, 15–16
   governors 8, 16, 128
   head teachers 8, 16
   non–teaching assistants 16, 59
   SEN Co-ordinator 16, 19, 55
   teaching staff 16
Room management 60, *Activity Pack 4*

SATs 36, 50
SCAA 36, 52
Schedule I Reg 2(1) 64, 100, *Appendix 2b*
School
   development plan 21, 100
   nurse 66, 70
   role in tribunal 84
SEN
   budget 9, 99
   construct 8, 15, **101–102**
   co–ordinator 13–15
   definition 8
   dilemmas 8–9, 14
   in-service 97
   management form 55, 79–80, *Appendix 8b*
   medical model of 71, 100
   policy 12, 13, 15, 20–21, *Source list 2*
   provision 16
   register 13, 23, 79–80
   social model of 70, 100

   support 55, 61
   tribunal 11, **84–85**, 95
SENCO
   as consultant 80
   development of co-ordinator role 17–18
   as manager 56
   multi-disciplinary development 68
   role of 19, 55, 97, 101–102
   support for 62, 97
   as supporter 61, 97
   support services liaison 68–71
   training for 18, 62, 100–102
   timetable 19
SENIOS 18
Service level agreements 65, 72
SNAP 27, 36, 40
Speech and language
   difficulties 48
   teachers 65
   therapists 48
Social services role 66–67, 70, 75
Soft systems methodology 100
Special schools 66
Stage *1* assessment & intervention 25–27, 30, 47–52
Stage *2* assessments & intervention 27–29, 31–32, 56
Stage *3* assessments & intervention 29–33, 81, 69–70
Stage *4* requests 69, **81–82**
Statements 12, 71, **82–84**
Appendices – *Appendix 8a*
Appendix D 82
   support 56–57, 60
   targets 71, 82
Support
   for child 56
   for curriculum 57
   for family 62
   guidelines 57
   management of 61
   specialist support 62
   services 64–65, 69–72
   for teacher 58

Task analysis 28, 40
Thinking skills 43
Training for
   teachers
   non-teaching assistants 59, 125
SENCOs 17, 62
Transition between phases 73–74
Transition plans 74–75
Triggers for assessment 11

Visually Impaired Service 65, 70
Voluntary organisations 66, 68, *Source list 3*
Warnock Report 8
Whole-school approach 13–20, 99–100
   policy review 20, *Activity Pack 2*

Zone of professional development 35